Building
Bussage

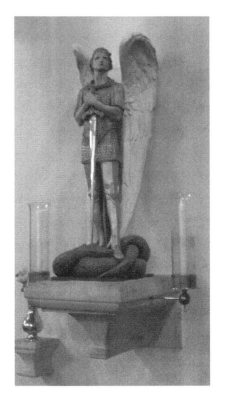

The history of St Michael and All Angels Church, Bussage

Written and Researched by
Patricia Main, BA (Hons) MA

Further copies of this book may be obtained from Amazon.com.

Foreword

When I embarked upon this history I had been living in this tiny corner of Gloucestershire for approximately four months. I knew nothing of its history, its people, and very little of its geography. But as I dug deeper into the research I discovered a wealth of little stories – some uplifting, some heartbreaking, all fascinating. Nobody would say that Bussage is in anyway important on the world stage, but, and this is a big but, the actions of the people who spent their lives here resonate both through history and across the world. I am a storyteller and I have endeavoured to tell the stories of the people who have acted out their lives on this stage, to bring them to life for a brief moment. I hope I have in some small way, achieved this aim, adding my contribution to the story that is Bussage.

Patricia Main, 09 March 2018

In Honorem Dei. Mortuorum et vivorum Domini

Thus says the LORD of hosts: "Consider your ways! Go up to the mountains and bring wood and build the temple, that I may take pleasure in it and be glorified," says the LORD.

Haggai ch 1 vv 7-8

Acknowledgement

Thanks are due to all the people who supplied information, especially Peter Clissold who lent me the wonderfully bound copies of the Parish Magazine and gave me snippets of information. Thanks also to Peter Drover of the Chalford Local History Group. My gratitude is equally due to all my friends who listened patiently while I enthused about the latest 'discovery' I had made while researching for this book. But my gratitude goes especially to Rev. Mike Clark for encouraging my efforts at accurately representing the lives of the residents of this tiny part of Gloucestershire. This history was entirely his idea … which is one way of saying, this is completely and utterly his fault!

All uncited photographs are either my own, entirely amateur handiwork or archive copies. The photos of the various clergy in Chapter 6 were all kindly supplied by Peter Drover of the Chalford Local History Group.

Contents

Chapter 1 - Bussage in the early 1800s

The [Tractarian] movement was one of moral and spiritual intensity rarely equalled, perhaps never surpassed. There was very little show about it. There was almost a contempt of elaboration in externals, as being too near akin to display. ... It may remind us of beginnings laid under cloudy skies, amidst dark forebodings, in profound humility, with the quiet courage of sure faith and reserved devotion.

Excerpt from page ii of the preface to
The Christian Year by Rev. John Keble

Bussage in the early part of the nineteenth century was a forlorn place, a place it would not be too fanciful perhaps to say lay 'under cloudy skies amidst dark forebodings'.

It was a small hamlet that, as Mary Rudd tells us in her history, 'included Eastcombe (... the combe of the ash-tree) and stretched south-wards as far as Black Ness to the Stroud valley. Bisley Common extended to Brownshill and bounded the tything on the east and the Todsmore stream marked the western side'[1]. But it was far from being a rural paradise; at the time we are studying, the early 1800s, the occupants of this tiny corner of England were seeing their centuries-old way of life crumble as modern economic and technological demands took their toll on the woollen industry that had been their lifeblood for generations.

---

[1] Rudd p338

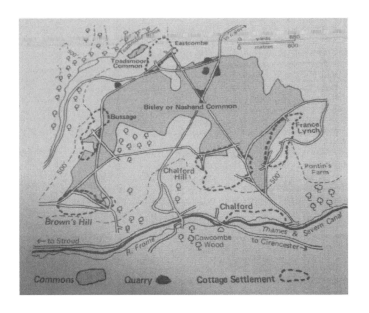

The tything of Bussage was a rambling, higgledy-piggledy community linked by footpaths and tracks - 'the upper road, dipping down to north Bussage near the Ram, and then running on to Bisley above Eastcombe,' [2] was not made until 1865 when the common was enclosed. Until then, the community was served by a road that ran north from Bussage House across Applegarth (then an orchard), up the lane and into the field below the vicarage before crossing the former allotments and entering Vatch Lane, up the lane and into the field where a track to Bisley can be traced across the fields to Eastcombe and Sheephouse. Around the beginning of the 19th century there were several cottages built along this track.

In the summary of a report on the plight of workers

[2] Rudd p338

8

in the woollen cloth trade made to Parliament in 1831 special note is made of the 'clothing establishments' at Chalford covering an area of approximately nine miles square which contained 90 mills. As the report states, 'the peculiar features of this district are the situation of the mills on streams in deep ravines; the scattered and irregular manner in which the houses are built on the hill sides; and the contrast between the high land (in many cases either wood or common with few inhabitants) and the vallies (sic), studded with houses and thickly peopled.' (p4 of the Summary). It should be noted that the area had no local Lord or person of wealth and influence to whom the local populace could look for support or assistance.

Place Names

There is some difference of opinion as to how the places in the area got their names. In a letter dated July 1896, Rev. Suckling wrote: 'I well remember the late revered Vicar of Bisley [The Rev. Thomas Keble] telling me of the derivation of the names of Bisley, Bussage and Bismore. In times gone by these places were celebrated for their abounding honey and were so called from this fact: Bisley was the field of bees; the edge of, or boundary of the bees, was Bussage, or Bees' edge, and Bees' more. I found not long back, in the British Museum, a notice of certain tithes being paid at Bisley in honey!'

However, Mary Rudd asserts that the name of Bussage comes 'from the Bysrugg of 1304 … and

Bussige in 1722' 'translated by the late Mr. G. J. Wood F.S.A., as "the ridge by the does" but modern experts would probably explain it as the ridge of Bissa.' [3] However, she goes on to say in her history that, 'in view of the numerous place names of the Cotswold district of old times indicating the animals of field or wood, perhaps many will accept the first interpretation'. Oxford College owned property in Chalford and, according to Rudd, their documents mention the 'woods of Bysrugge' and the Faber family of Bysrige (mid 14th century).

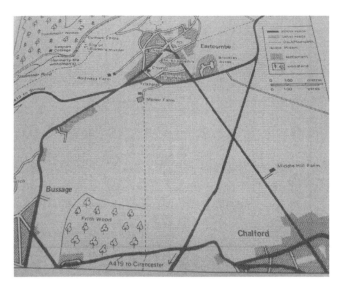

A Weaving Armageddon

The Stroud area had been renowned for the high

---

[3] Rudd p338

quality of its workmanship in a country justly famed for woollen cloth since mediaeval times. Daniel Defoe writes in the mid-1700s of 'a most pleasant and fruitful vale ... which is called Stroud-Water; famous not for the finest cloths only, but for dying those cloths of the finest scarlets, and other grain colours that are any where in England ... the clothiers lie all along the banks of this river for near 20 miles'.[4] 'The Stroud region became famous for several speciality products and was especially noted for its "Stroud Scarlets"; these were regarded as the finest reds in England and were frequently used for the manufacture of military uniforms'[5]. Wool was the basis of most of the prosperity in the area, providing a comfortable lifestyle for the many craftsmen employed in the various processes required to convert the raw fleece into the finished cloth.

It is perhaps worthy of note that the impressive estate at Lypiatt Park was owned in 1802 by Paul Wathan, a local clothier, and in 1824 by William Lewis, a Brimscombe clothier. Clearly the cloth industry was generating substantial profits.

Prior to the mechanisation of the weaving industry 'a handloom weaver worked in his home, his wife and family helping him. He was free to work the hours he chose ... he might grow vegetables, keep pigs or run a few sheep on the common which would all provide him with a change of scene and a breath of

[4] Defoe p 367/8

[5] Mills p20

fresh air'.[6]   The highly skilled craft of weaving took approximately four years to learn and was very much a family business with fathers passing on their skills to their sons. 'The children of weavers would help by winding the quills, which went into the shuttles. By watching and helping, they often imperceptibly picked up enough knowledge to start weaving themselves when they were old enough'[7]

Plaque from Bisley Churchyard dated 1711 commemorating a local Clothier and his wife.

The key processes in the manufacture of a piece of broadcloth were:
- Wool Preparation:
    - scouring with urine (known as seg) at the clothier's premises
    - Picking by the willy or devil to open

[6] Lambert & Shipman p23

[7] Lambert & Shipman p25

the fibres
- o Dyeing (for some cloths)when dry
- Yarn manufacture:
  - o Willying
  - o Scribbling
  - o carding : a carding machine consisting of rollers covered with wire was patented as early as 1748, it wasn't until the 1790s that improved versions were widely adopted
  - o slubbing
  - o spinning: the early jenny was hand-operated but it wasn't long before clothiers began to install them at mills. By the 1820s some spinning jennies in Gloucestershire had 80 spindles
- Weaving:
  - o warping: winding out the warp yarn into a 'chain' for the weaver
  - o sizing: covering the warp with size – a form of glue
  - o weaving: while the flying shuttle was adopted in Yorkshire from the 1760s, it doesn't appear to have reached Gloucestershire until the 1790s, probably because Yorkshire looms were narrow and Gloucestershire ones broad. Some of the larger clothiers built hand-loom weaving shops at their mills
- Finishing:
  - o Scouring
  - o fulling/milling: the fulling process

remained more or less unchanged, using stocks, until the 1840s when the milling machine was introduced. After fulling, the cloth was stretched on racks on the valley sides to dry, although by the 1830s a number of the larger mills had 'air stoves' – long cloth drying rooms which were ventilated by the circulation of air

- o gigging
- o shearing: hand shearing required huge skill and shearman was the highest-paid of all textile craftspeople. The first patents for improvements were granted at the end of the 18th century and many patents were taken out by local men in the period to 1825

• Dyeing and pressing: some dying was undertaken by the larger clothiers and some by independent dyers such as Bowbridge Dyeworks, Peter Watts of Wallbridge, and Hawkers at Dudbridge, all of whom dyed on commission, usually specialising in particular colours. Hot pressing gave a gloss to the cloth; a patent being taken out for the process by John and William Lewis, of Brimscombe, with William Davis in 1819.

(Extract from Stroud Textile.org website) Although several of these operations were carried out in mills or factories, many continued to be done on out-workers' premises. How was this achieved? Possibly, as E. Lipson suggests in his history of the woollen and worsted trade, because the clothiers of the Gloucestershire area negotiated the change better than their northern counterparts in overcoming the opposition to machinery.

As a result, the resistance that culminated in the infamous Luddite attacks and subsequent arrests and trials that occurred in the north of the country were not mirrored here, though there was some civil unrest as will be seen. The situation was that, despite the fact that vast cloth mills had been constructed in the Stroud area during the 1790s, right up to the mid-1820s weaving continued to be a mainly cottage-based industry where master weavers employed journeymen and apprentices on a small scale, frequently working in buildings close to their homes, if not actually in their own homes.

A clothier would employ cottage-based workers who supplied the necessary spinning and weaving with self-employed fullers and dyers finishing the cloth, but this was starting to change as larger and larger mills were constructed – one in Stonehouse in 1812 was a five-storey building with a working space on each floor of some 185 sq metres (2,000 sq ft) accommodating over eighteen spinning jennies each with eighty spindles as well as weaving sheds and dye houses of a comparable size. The cloth produced by machine was of a more consistent quality than that made by the hand-weavers and it made commercial sense for the clothiers to collect all the processes under one roof, so to speak, where it could be under their control and where they could better regulate the finances. But 'despite its industrialization in the early nineteenth century, the Gloucester woollen industry failed to sustain continuous economic growth. Having passed from the putting-out [cottage industry] to the factory system, the industry declined because its clothiers failed to implement key innovations effectively'[8].

Clothiers wanting to keep a closer eye on their weavers had installed looms in factory buildings and this changed the whole way of life of the men and women who worked in the industry. The crunch came in 1824 when a coalition of factory owners not only demanded a more consistent quality of end product from the remaining independent workers but also increased the size of a woven piece to match that produced by their machines, which effectively reduced the price paid for their work. The master weavers who, until this point had apparently considered their craft to be safe, as evidenced by their taking on and training a large number of apprentices, rebelled. They had seen their respect as craftsmen eroded by the introduction of machinery and, reluctantly, accepted it, but the financial impact of these alterations was one step too far. The legitimacy of an employer's authority had been based on the concept of mutual obligation and respect. Now that employers appeared to be failing in their duties to their workers (by reducing pay and arbitrarily changing conditions), the system collapsed.

On 29 April 1825, the master weavers went on strike. 'The weavers' committee succeeded in mobilizing followers from all parishes in both Stroud and lower districts'[9]. 6,000 weavers gathered on Selsey Hill on

[8] Urdank p195

16

11th May to hear what the manufacturers would say in response to their demands for fairer prices, but too few manufacturers were willing to agree these terms, many Stroud clothiers claiming that their contracts with the East India Company prevented them from raising prices.

Threatened by action from the Tenth Hussars then based in Bristol, the weavers of the lower district agreed to return to work on 18th May but, whilst some clothiers fell in with the demands, one-third of the manufacturers in Stroud refused to accept the weavers' prices and some even went so far as to close their works in protest.

The strike turned violent at the beginning of June. 'A crowd descended on the Wyatts at Vatch mills … which led to a scuffle, and ultimately to a complete riot'[10]. The Wyatt brothers were assaulted and beaten, and eight of their men, who had been appointed as special constables to police the gathering, were attacked and ducked in the Vatch mill pond. The Hussars duly put in an appearance on 6th June but by then the riots had stopped, although vast numbers of workers were still to be seen milling around the streets of Stroud.

Subsequent trials of rioters suggest that the magistrates were sympathetic to the weavers' plight. Possibly because, unlike the Luddite riots in the north of the country, there was little or no violence

[9] Urdank p214

[10] Urdank p216

against machinery or property and, apart from the duckings which did occur in several places, little against people either.

However, this period of unrest and change in the culture and working practice of the local population had severe social consequences: in December 1825 a number of country banks failed and as the resultant economic depression bit, unemployment soared.

Lodgemoor mill in Stroud, originally owned by the Cooke family but in financial difficulties by 1827, it changed hands several times

By 1826, a third of the population of Bisley parish was unemployed … and the situation worsened - 'out of a total population of around 6000 in Bisley, only 658 were in full work'[11]. There was widespread unemployment in the area as mill after mill went out of business as a result of the collapse of the woollen

---

[11] Stroud Textile.org

market in the 1830s and, by 1839, twenty-six of the forty-one mills in Chalford had closed. One writer tells us that "in the county of Gloucester fifty years ago (i.e. 1750) the clothing business flourished to a very great extent, but afterwards migrated in a considerable degree to Yorkshire, where the price of labour was less, the necessaries of life cheaper, and the actual wealth had not produced indolence. In consequence of this decline the populous parishes of Bisley, Horsley, Stroud, and others in those enchanting vales, fell into decay, and almost wholly into beggary. I cannot forget the colonies of mendicants which, thirty years ago, poured from them into the adjacent towns on the Cotswold Hills. If you asked a beggar from the first of those parishes whence he came, it was common, even to a proverb, for him to answer: 'From Bisley – God help!''[12]

One of the many footpaths in winter that were the only means of getting around the parish

'By 1830, it was now necessary for the whole family

[12] Lipson p?

to work. Many of the men, women and children were away at work from early in the morning until eight or nine o'clock at night'[13]. It was not just a question of machines in factories taking the work previously undertaken by craftsmen in cottages, the alteration also removed their independence; the master weavers lost respect both in the community and for themselves, as they became 'slaves' working twelve hour shifts in poor conditions which also deprived them of the time to tend animals and grow food. It is no surprise that some claimed: 'they have driven us from our houses and gardens to work as prisoners in their factories'[14].

It is easy to see how the installation of power looms and the incorporation of all aspects of the industry under one roof impacted on what had been, up until then, a cottage industry, utterly destroying the way of life of families of craftsmen and women. The subsequent failure of these businesses – '133 Gloucestershire woollen mills were recorded at work in 1831; and the number had fallen to 77 by 1841. Some 15 manufacturers failed between 1835 and 1841'[15] – and the migration of the market to the mills in the north of the country, merely exacerbated an already untenable situation.

In his history of St Michael and All Angels, Michael Lambert describes the condition of the Bussage

---

[13] Lambert & Shipman p26

[14] Lambert & Shipman p23

[15] Stroud Textile.org

population during this period in graphic detail:

Handloom weavers in the cheapest cottages hung on to their independence at the cost of marginal diet, breakfast of bread and warm water flavoured with a little salt and pepper, dinner of potatoes with "flick" (fat) poured on them.[16]

The factory workers had little or no time to spend on growing their own food and were forced to use the 'shops by factories, covertly linked to the owners'[17]. Needless to say, the food sold in these outlets was not of the best quality and there were reports of rotten meat being sold to workers. 'One way in which some manufacturers sought to continue in business was through the payment of truck – payment in kind or in vouchers. This was particularly prevalent in Chalford.'[18] It is perhaps relevant to note that 1846 was the height of the potato famine in Ireland so reports of starving people were not news and there was little support for those teetering on the edge of survival.

Mary Rudd describes the inhabitants of the area as 'very rough and ignorant and the standard of morals and general conduct was very low'[19] and she cites the lack of a school or church as at least part of the reason for this. The parish church at Bisley and a

[16] Lambert p2

[17] Ibid

[18] Stroud Textile.org

[19] Rudd p362

chapel in Chalford formed the only Anglican presence in the area and that had little impact on the scattered and impoverished population. Lambert and Shipman state that 'there were 16 paupers in the village [Eastcombe] in 1851 and about thirty villagers used to receive annual gifts of blankets, shirts and yards of linen from Bisley charities'[20].

Clearly, provision of pastoral care had not improved since Bishop Benson's Survey which was undertaken in the mid-1700s and which reported on page 50 that 'the inhabitants of Chalford and its vicinities are estimated at near two thousand, who are above two miles distant from the parish church'. In a society where the only state welfare was the workhouse, the work of the various religious denominations in rural areas like this was vital in supporting the population. This was the world that Rev. Thomas Keble moved into when he was appointed Vicar of Bisley in 1827.

The People

So who were the people living in Bussage in the early 1800s? Here are a few snippets of information supplied by Mary Rudd and other sources as shown:

- Bussage house was purchased by William Toghill from John Yale in 1826, though he doesn't appear to have lived in it and put in John Drew as tenant. A later owner, William Davis

---

[20] Lambert and Shipman p26

(known as Squire Davis) enlarged the house, adding a large room at the back for use by the Baptists as a meeting place. The house was converted into a boys' school by John Sibree and it continued as a school until F J Sibree, then running it, left the parish after being ordained in 1898 and taking a parish in Norfolk. (Parish Magazine Dec. 1898)

- Squire Davis also owned Woodlands, St Michael's Cottage (aka Bussage Villa) which was originally a farmhouse and the orchard, Applegarth. Woodlands was originally two cottages, one being a Dame School. After her husband's death Mrs Suckling rented Woodlands.

- The Old House – originally built for Henry Collins, a broadweaver - was inherited by Thomas Collins and mortgaged in 1725. He sold it to William Long and by 1816 it had been assigned to Samuel Rogers recorded as being a victualler. 'The Old House is then described as having a shop' (Rudd p343)

- The Ram Inn, 'formerly a picturesque old cottage covered with creepers, bearing the date 1800' (Rudd p344) was rebuilt in 1900.

The Ram Inn, date unknown (Peter Drover)

The 1841 census shows Anne Rogers (aged 55) as the publican. William Alley (40 yrs) is also shown as a publican in the census but he does not live at The Ram and his home is not designated as an inn.

- In 1826 Richard Jefferies was living in a cottage in what was formerly the garden of Bussage Vicarage; it was later occupied by the Armstrong family.

The 1841 census also gives us a fascinating snapshot of life in Bussage – giving us names, ages, family groupings, occupations and, by deduction, an intimation of education and status. Covering the area from the top of Vatch Lane to Frith, and incorporating an area called Blinki which no-one appears to be able to identify, the census return is packed with information about the people who were living in Bussage when the church was built. Some of their tombstones may be seen in the churchyard.

A summary of the data shows that there were 43 households in the area and seven empty houses. A total of 250 souls are registered.

There are 17 agricultural labourers, aged between 13 and 70:

!st Name	Surname	Age
William	Munday	75
Zeckeria	Davis	70
William	Tanner	70
Charlie	Alley	45
Thomas	Strong	40
William	Wright	40
Isaac	Hunt	35
Nathan	Pincott	35
John	Wright	30
William	Munday	20
William	Davis	20
John	Philpot	20
Henery	Lervis	16
Charles	Davis	15
Joseph	Alley	15
John	Butler	14
Samuel	Hunt	13

68 people work in the wool trade, the youngest being Thomas Fawkes (5 yrs – a carder)) and Samuel Smith (8 yrs – factory); the oldest Charles Freeman (63 – a carder), James Young (60) and Thomas Lee (weavers) and Anne Smith (50 – working in the factory)

35 are employed in other ways, including: bargeman, dressmaker, cordwinder, farrier, patten clogmaker, iron founder, joiner, stone mason, waterman, school mistress and one John Whiting – constable.

Of the 75 children (i.e. under 12 years of age) 2 work in the woollen industry (see above).

Finally, 25 individuals are shown as having 'independent means'.

For readers fascinated by demographics, the following is a breakdown of the population by age:

infants	4
Under 12	71
Aged 12-20	46
Aged 20-30	30
Aged 30-40	27
Aged 40-50	33
Aged 50-60	21
Aged 60-70	10
Aged 70-80	7
Over 80	1

A wander around the churchyard shows headstones for some of those mentioned in the Census of 1841:
- John Wright who is shown as an Agricultural labourer, and Harriat Wright, a weaver. Harriat was buried at the age of 55 in January 1860, and John was buried in August 1867 when he was 64

years of age. Although it is not clear from their tombstone that they were husband and wife, after all it is possible they could have been siblings, the long list of children – Anne (13), Joshua (10), Dinah (7), George (5) and Adeline (2) - shown in the census overwhelmingly suggests that they were married.

- Married couple, Thomas and Jemima Marmont, were both mill workers in 1841 – she died on 27th June 1878 aged 83 and he a few years later on 29th January 1881 aged 82. The census shows that they had two daughters, Eizabeth and Mary, in 1841.

There are doubtless many more but the poor quality of the stones used to mark the graves and the weathering over the time that has passed since their erection has obliterated the details.

The Parish Magazine which was started in 1895 has a report written in February 1900 by Rev. R A J Suckling (son of Rev. Robert Suckling, first incumbent of St Michael & All Angels) in which he mentions life as he remembered it growing up in Bussage.

He recalls John Bird was the Bussage Shoemaker "and his efforts to be a witness for God in that spot that he called "the God-forsaken spot". Then he goes on to mention William Davis (there was a large number of Davises and several of them shared the name 'William' – a researcher's nightmare!) who, with his two sisters, Mary and Martha, lived in 'the Cave on the Common' before building and moving into a house which he called 'The Palace'. Nostalgically, Suckling remembers with obvious pleasure that 'we had our lovely Common (you have lost that) and we used to play cricket on that well-known spot in front of Jehoiada Witt's house'.

But despite the doom and gloom clouding the picture of Bussage in the early part of the 19th century, the arrival of Rev. Keble and the changes that he effected had great impact. So much so that a note in the August 1898 edition of the Parish Magazine favourably compares the then current conditions in the parish (i.e. 1898) with the Bussage of 1848:

In the Bussage of fifty years ago, how many persons could have been found able to read or write or how many were there who had been ten miles from their homes? The number of either would be very small indeed, whereas now there is scarcely one who cannot read his Magazine, or write ... and there are comparatively few who have not, at some time or other, travelled to places in other parts of England which their fathers would have considered as far beyond their means as Africa or America is nowadays.

These improvements continued and by 1900, Rev. Macleod is able to write in the Parish Magazine: 'when the History of English Village Life in the Nineteenth Century comes to be written, it will be found that better Education and improved facilities for Travel have affected it to an extent unknown in any like period of earlier times'. There is even a suggestion that the workers in the mills are by that time enjoying staff outings … 'the annual Summer Outings in which so many of us share, either through connection with the Mills or as associated with some Parochial organisation' being a part of community life which would have been unknown fifty years previously.

Chapter 2 - Thomas Keble – the man

The Reverend Thomas Keble was 34 years of age when he was instituted to the parish of Bisley in 1827. Described by Dean Church as a man with strong, definite opinions on all subjects who could be curt and intolerant of anything that he saw as threatening the 'wholesome teaching and interests of the church', he 'exemplified the virtues of simplicity, a calm sense of duty and humble resignation'[21]. As the biography on the Bisley website states: 'his whole life [was] one of concern for his parish and people'.

So who was this man who was to have such an impact on the parish of Bisley? His background was one of privilege and comfort.

Born on 25th October 1793 to Sarah, wife of the Rev. John Keble then Vicar of Coln St Aldwyns some nine miles east of Cirencester, he was educated by his father at home until 1808 when, at the age of fifteen, he went up to Oxford as Gloucestershire scholar of Corpus Christi College.

He does not appear to have been a particularly gifted

[21] Torode p 14

scholar, achieving a second in Classics and a third in mathematics, however, this did not prevent him from following his chosen career in the Church. Perhaps following his father's example, he was ordained deacon in December 1816 and priested a year later. Sadly, his first posting as curate of Sherborne with Windrush, Gloucestershire, was short-lived as a series of serious illnesses forced him back to Oxford where, in the autumn of 1819 he became a tutor at his old college.

The next few years saw him steadily rising through the ranks of Oxford scholarship and by the time he left to take up a curacy in Cirencester – his status now that of Junior Dean - he had also acquired a Batchelor of Divinity degree. Whilst at Oxford he shared the curacy of Eastleach Turville and Eastleach Martin (near Fairford) with his elder brother John, also an ordained priest.

But Thomas Keble was no poor curate; he had, so Torode tells us, inherited money from an uncle and was financially secure, if not relatively wealthy. His marriage to Elizabeth Jane Clarke followed on 14 June 1824. Elizabeth was the elder daughter of Rev. George Clarke, an old friend of Keble's family, and Rector of Meysey Hampton (near Cirencester). Her sister married Thomas Keble's brother, John, and a stained glass window in the south aisle of Bisley Church commemorates the marriage there of John Keble and Charlotte Clarke on 10th October 1835. Thomas officiated at this event - a circumstance that demonstrates clearly the closeness of the two brothers.

According to the information on the Bisley benefice website, Thomas and Elizabeth had three daughters (two of whom married clergy) and a son, Thomas, who followed the family tradition by going into the priesthood; in fact, he took over from his father as Vicar of Bisley in 1873.

Bisley was Thomas Keble's first incumbency but his experience both at one remove, as a child of his father, and later as a curate had given him a wealth of understanding of what the role of a parish priest ought to be. One can only imagine the conversations that must have taken place within the walls of the vicarage as he and Elizabeth (a daughter of a Vicar!) discussed the plight of their new parishioners – the problems caused by the collapse of the woollen industry, the working conditions in the mills that had replaced the thriving cottage industry, the lack of alternative employment in the area and what they could do about any or all of these problems.

An old trackway on the way to Stroud – very pretty but not on foot in bad weather!

The mere challenge of physically getting around the

small hamlets scattered in the hills and valleys that comprised the parish, where roads were few and poverty haunted the homes of the people, cannot have improved the health of Keble who suffered from ill-health for much of his life. A lesser man would perhaps have concluded that the task was too great, but Thomas Keble was made of sterner stuff.

A scrap of paper held in the Gloucester Archives notes Keble's ongoing attentiveness to the condition of his parishioners though for what purpose is not known. The population of Bisley is scrawled as follows:

Population of Bisley in 1841

Males	2520
Females	2798
Total	5318
Canal	14
Total	5332

He took an interest in every aspect of village life even to the beautification of the bank by the Wells (Springs) in Bisley. Amongst his correspondence held at the Gloucester Archives is a list of the trees he suggests for planting here:

'Divided into deciduous and evergreens and flowering shrubs including silver firs, broom white and yellow, cotoneaster, weeping willow, and for the borders next to the yard: yew, cyprus, red cedar, common laurel, Portugal laurel, tree box, guelders rose, ribes, lilac, syringa,'.

There is also a letter from Louisa Champernoune of

Vineyard dated Sept 20 1854 and addressed to Mrs Keble which refers to this:

My dear Mrs Keble, I shall be very glad to give £20 ... for the Springs ... The morning was very wet here but it is a beautiful evening. Yours very affectionately, Louisa Champernoune

This minute example demonstrates, if somewhat prosaically, the way that Keble and his wife worked together for the benefit of the parish.

Keble was a man of many parts and other correspondence retained at the Gloucester Archives includes items relating to his antiquarian interests and a fascinating letter claiming to explain the names of places local to Gloucestershire with reference to Hebrew and Greek.

Practical Churchmanship

In accordance with his Tractarian stance – by this time he had written four Tracts submitted for publication in The Times – Thomas Keble instituted daily Prayer Book services in the church with Matins at 10 a.m. and Evening Prayer at 4 p.m. Bishop Askwith is quoted in Torode's notes as saying in 1960 that 'when Thomas Keble arrived in Bisley he probably shook the people by going to church every day. Although regarded as not quite respectable and causing a great deal of resentment in many places around, Thomas Keble and others brought about a great revival in church life for which we are still thanking God today.'

However, when Thomas Keble arrived 1827 the parish began to change. Not only did the new incumbent attract a number of notable curates - Sir George Prevost, Isaac Williams, Henry Jeffreys, William Lowder (the former architect) and many others who honed their craft under his tutelage at Bisley - but he used his own personal friends and resources to provide schools and churches in the villages.

Keble had no qualms about actively dealing with problems in his parish; on one occasion he threw out of church a falsely devout clothier whom he knew maltreated his wife. He also encouraged girls from the local orphanage to attend.

Within two years of his arrival, not satisfied with merely changing the shape of services and worship in Bisley church, he began an enormous and highly ambitious building programme:

1829   The repair of the spire of All Saints', Bisley
1832   A new vicarage in Bisley
1837   The building of St Bartholomew's church at Oakridge, along with a vicarage and school (consecrated 1837)
1841   The enlargement of Chalford Chapel into Christ Church and Chalford Parish instituted as a separate entity (achieved in 1841)
1846   The building of St Michael and All Angels church in Bussage (consecrated in 1846)
1857   The building of St John the Baptist church,

France Lynch (consecrated 1857)

1862   The restoration of All Saints' church, Bisley
       – despite some opposition from parishioners
       this was achieved in 1862!

1868   The building of a school, chapel and school
       house in Eastcombe as well as other schools
       for the new parishes (1868)

In 1837 he also organised the emigration of 68 of his impoverished parishioners to Sydney, Australia. They were provided with transport to Bristol, clothing and food, in addition to which Keble presented each family with a Bible and Prayer Book. Examples of these are on display in Bisley Church (see photo below) where a document shows the cost to the parish of their 'emigration' amounted to £191 3s and 1d – approximately £15,000 in today's money.

However, the hamlet of Eastcombe presented Keble

with a problem. During the 1800s the Church of England in the guise of the previous incumbent had virtually ignored the village; the then Vicar of Bisley (1782-1806) had lived in Somerset and rarely visited the area. As a result of this neglect not only was Bisley Vicarage little more than a ruin but, according to Torode, Eastcombe was 'a hard-bitten, godless place'. The Baptist Chapel had been built in 1801 and prospered; perhaps as a result of this, there were few Anglicans living in the village.

Though only one and a quarter miles from the parish church in Bisley, Eastcombe was a stronghold of the Baptists so Keble moved quietly using his curate and former architect, William Lowder, brother of Charles Fuge Lowder, to build a house in the village for an Anglican schoolteacher (now Church House) and next door to it a church school. There is a roundel with the date 1868 above one of the western buttresses. The school became an improvised church on Sundays and in 1876 services were held there on a Wednesday evening. In 1877 an altar was set up at the east end behind folding doors. On Sundays, these doors were pulled back, a font and lectern rolled out and desks turned round to make seating for sixty people, as opposed to the 700 available at the Baptist Chapel. One of Thomas Keble's daughters helped with needlework in the school.

However, one Baptist minister objected to his flock sending their children to the school where 'they were taught that they were not part of the true church' so the Baptists set up their own school. When the Baptist school was opened in 1878 the guest of honour was Sir Samuel Morton Riho, the Liberal MP, who denounced the heretical teaching and priestly pretensions of the High Church Party and urged the non-conformists to stem the torrent of ritualism and unbelief.

As a result there was much antagonism in the village with rival pupils calling one another 'church dumps' or 'chapel dumps'. Despite this Keble persisted, he chose Ascension Day as Well Dressing Day and Eastcombe children were invited to join in. What the reaction to this may have been is not recorded!

Thomas Keble died on 5th September 1875. His funeral began at 8 am with Holy Communion. There was then a breakfast followed by Morning Service at 10 am and a burial service at the graveside. It is a monument to the respect in which he was held that his coffin was accompanied by six of his former curates and a seventh officiated. The service was supported by a choir, with three psalms, Venite, Te Deum, Benediction, an anthem, a Hymn and a Canticle. Eight aged parishioners acted as bearers although the Pall was supported by six former curates – Gregory, Jeffreys, Frith (Vicar of Coalpit Heath) Livingstone (Vicar of Forthampton) W.H. Lowder (by then, Vicar of Alverley, Cheshire); Rev Isaac Williams, curate of Stinchcombe. The service was conducted by Sir G. Prevost.

Thomas Keble was succeeded at Bisley by his son Thomas 1873-1903.

As can be seen from this advertisement in The Musical Times edition of 1st October 1873, Thomas Keble was sufficiently well known for his suggestions regarding the use of the Te Deum in church services to be a selling point for a set of chants for this text. Something generations of choristers will be familiar with.

TE DEUM LAUDAMUS, Set to Original Chants, price 2d., composed by FREDERICK ILIFFE, Mus. Bac., Oxon., Fellow of the College of Organists, London.

" In writing these Chants for the Te Deum I have divided it into its doctrinal parts. The 'first' thirteen verses are a Creed setting forth the doctrine of the Trinity. The 'second' part beginning with the words ' Thou art the King of glory,' and the four following verses, set forth the Divinity and Incarnation of the Son. The solemn verse 'We believe that Thou shalt come,' expresses our belief in our Lord's second coming. A separate Chant is provided for this verse. The 'third' part, beginning with the words ' We therefore pray Thee ' is a Litany.

" The Rev. Thomas Keble was the first, I believe, who suggested this ancient mode of dividing the Te Deum into these several parts, and I have adhered to this arrangement as far as possible; there is, how- ever, one exception, and that is in the first part of the verse, ' Holy, Holy, Holy,' which seems to me to demand a different kind of expression to any of the other verses. I may also say that I had written another Chant of a more pensive character for the ' Litany part,' but it was thought advisable to go back to the melody of the first Chant, in order to avoid many changes."—*Prefatory Remarks by the Composer.*

Keble's Curates and Associates:

Isaac Williams: In 1842 Isaac Williams left Oxford for Bisley where he was to be curate to Thomas Keble until 1848. He too had served his first curacy at Windrush and in 1833 he aligned himself with the Oxford Movement. Williams became a True Blue Tractarian and his family built a model Tractarian Church at Llangorwen near Aberystwyth.

It was at Bisley that he married Caroline, the third daughter of Arthur Champernowne (and sister of Rev. Richard Champernowne, curate of Oakridge) in 1842. He had first proposed to her in 1827 when she was only 16 but his proposals had been thwarted by Richard Froude, one of the Oxford Movement's primary movers and shakers). Although this must have hurt at the time, Williams later admitted he was grateful otherwise he would have lost the opportunity of working both at Windrush and at Oxford with Newman.

Isaac Williams went on to become curate at Newman's church (St Mary and St Nicholas, Littlemore near Oxford) and when Newman went abroad leaving Williams in charge, he introduced daily services there. Parish life was his main interest.

He presented a stone altar to Bisley in 1851 after he'd moved to Stinchcombe, following Sir George, in 1848. The cost of this was defrayed from the proceeds of his 'Plain Sermons'. Whilst in Stinchcombe he contributed greatly towards the restoration of the church, doubtless inspired by Keble's example in Bisley, and was buried there in 1865.

A close friend of Rev. Robert Suckling (the first priest to hold the parish at St Michael & All Angels, Bussage) he later produced a Memoir of Suckling based on the journals written by Suckling himself; a copy of this his held at Gloucester County Archives.

Henry Jeffreys: During the years 1835-36 influenza devastated parish of Bisley and Keble's curate Henry Jeffreys went around the parish feeding people with toast dipped in port wine. £600 was collected to enable the poor and unemployed to move to other parishes in search of work (cp the Australia project mentioned before). Mrs Keble sold rice and other foods at half price in her vicarage shed.

John Henry Newman: A close friend of both the Keble brothers, in 1837 Newman dined at Bisley with the Bishop and criticised the luxurious dinner provided by his host during such a time of poverty.

Chapter 3 - The Oxford Movement

The Oxford Movement appears to have been a spiritual reaction to the movements sweeping through literature and art during the 19th century. Often thought of as an attempt at Catholic revival in the Church of England, although several of the leading proponents were violently opposed to the Roman Catholic church, perhaps it could more accurately be defined as referring to the activities and ideas of an initially small group of people in the University of Oxford who argued against the increasing secularisation of the Church of England. They sought to recall the Church of England to its heritage of apostolic order and to the catholic doctrines of the early church fathers. This movement lead to two distinct offshoots: those who were given the name Tractarians and amongst whom the Keble brothers are numbered, and the wider Anglo-Catholic wing of the church which came about through the development of their ideas.

It began in the early 1830s at Oriel College in Oxford, where a growing number of young and extremely able Fellows, informally grouped around the slightly older John Keble, became increasingly outspoken about the needs and shortcomings of the contemporary church. These were heady times in England. Catholic emancipation had arrived and the forces surrounding the Reform Act of 1832 were being felt in all walks of life. Some thought that the old status quo was being threatened, but many questions about church government and doctrine were being left unanswered. There was a feeling that there was everything to play for.

John Henry Newman, Vicar of the University Church of St Mary the Virgin, Richard Hurrell Froude, a junior fellow of Oriel, and William Palmer, a fellow of Worcester, joined with Keble to launch a series of Tracts for the Times, developing these themes (hence the name Tractarians). During the following eight years, ninety such Tracts were published that questioned the very heart of Anglicanism.[22]

Leading Figures in the Oxford Movement

In Dean Church's words, the leading figures of the Oxford movement were 'men of large designs'. So who were these men? Taking them in alphabetical order …

Richard Hurrell Froude (25 March 1803 – 28 February 1836) was born in Dartington, Devon, the eldest son of Robert Froude (Archdeacon of Totnes) and the elder brother of historian James Anthony Froude and engineer and naval architect William Froude. He was educated at Ottery St Mary School, Eton College and Oriel College, Oxford, where he became a fellow in 1826.

At Oxford he became a close friend of John Keble and John Henry Newman, with whom he collaborated on the *Lyra Apostolica*, a collection of religious poems. He spent the winter of 1832–33

[22] All these tracts are available on the internet:
https://en.wikipedia.org/wiki/Tracts_for_the_Times .

travelling in the Mediterranean with his father and Newman for the sake of his health (he suffered from tuberculosis), contributing on his return to the formation of the Oxford Movement.

Much of the rest of his life was spent outside England in an attempt to alleviate his medical condition; he acted as mathematical tutor at Codrington College in the Barbados. However, he returned to England in 1835 and died from tuberculosis the following year. After his death, Newman and other friends edited the *Remains*, a collection of Froude's letters and journals. These were later interpreted by Sir Geoffrey Faber in his work *Oxford Apostles*, published in 1933 for the centenary of the Oxford Movement.

John Keble (25 April 1792 – 29 March 1866) was born in Fairford, Gloucestershire where his father, the Rev. John Keble, was Vicar of Coln St. Aldwyns. He attended Corpus Christi College, Oxford, and, after a brilliant academic performance there, became a Fellow of Oriel College, Oxford, and was for some years a tutor and examiner in the University. In 1815, while still at Oxford he took Holy Orders, and became, firstly, a curate to his father and, later, curate of St Michael and St Martin's Church, Eastleach Martin in Gloucestershire. Keble College, Oxford was named after him.

John Keble c. 1860

His book - '**The Christian Year**' – was published in 1827, and met with an almost unparalleled acceptance. Though at first published anonymously, its authorship soon became known, with the result that in 1831 Keble was appointed to the Chair of Poetry at Oxford, a post he held until 1841.

Victorian scholar Michael Wheeler calls *The Christian Year* simply "the most popular volume of verse in the nineteenth century". Not only that, but as Gregory Goodwin claims, *The Christian Year* is "Keble's greatest contribution to the Oxford Movement and to English literature." Ninety-five editions of this devotional text were printed during Keble's lifetime, and "at the end of the year following his death, the number had arisen to a hundred-and-nine". By the time the copyright expired in 1873, over 375,000 copies had been sold in Britain and 158 editions had been published.

In 1833 he gave his famous Assize Sermon on "National Apostasy" which led to the formation of the Oxford Movement. The subject matter of this sermon may seem remote: a protest against parliamentary legislation to reduce the absurdly large number of bishoprics in the Church of Ireland. But the theme was crucial - was the Church of England a department of the Hanoverian state, to be governed by the forces of secular politics, or was it an ordinance of God. Were its pastors priests of the Catholic Church (as the Prayer Book insisted) or ministers of a Calvinistic sect?

Keble became a leading light in the movement, as did his brother, Thomas, also active in the Oxford Movement and to whom he was extremely close. In 1835 John Keble was appointed Vicar of Hursley, Hampshire, where he settled down to family life and remained for the rest of his life as a parish priest at All Saints' Church.

John Henry Newman (21 February 1801 – 11 August 1890) was born in the City of London, the eldest of a family of three sons and three daughters. His father, John Newman, was a banker with Ramsbottom, Newman and Company in Lombard Street. His mother, Jemima (née Fourdrinier), was descended from a notable family of Huguenot refugees in England, founded by the engraver, printer and stationer Paul Fourdrinier. His eldest sister, Harriet Elizabeth, married Thomas Mozley, also prominent in the Oxford Movement.

On 13 June 1824, Newman was made an Anglican deacon in Christ Church Cathedral, Oxford and on Trinity Sunday, 29 May 1825, he was ordained a priest in Christ Church Cathedral by the Bishop of Oxford, Edward Legge. He became, at Pusey's suggestion, curate of St Clement's Church, Oxford. In 1826 he returned to Oriel College and met Richard Froude, described by Newman as "one of the acutest, cleverest and deepest men" he had ever met.

Together they created an ideal of the tutorial office as clerical and pastoral rather than secular, which led to tensions in the college. His name was known nationally by the mid-1830s.

Newman became known as a leader of, and an able campaigner for, the Oxford Movement.

William Palmer (12 July 1811 – 04 April 1879) was an English theologian and antiquarian, an Anglican priest and a fellow of Magdalen College, Oxford who examined the practicability of intercommunion between the Anglican and Orthodox churches. Like Newman, he later became a Roman Catholic. He actively pursued the building of a relationship with the Russian and Greek Orthodox Churches and visited Russia twice in unsuccessful pursuit of this aim.

Edward Bouverie Pusey (22 August 1800 – 16 September 1882) was an English churchman, for more than fifty years Regius Professor of Hebrew at Christ Church, Oxford. He was one of the leaders of the Oxford Movement**.**

In 1823 Pusey was elected by competition to a fellowship at Oriel College, Oxford where John Henry Newman and John Keble were already there as fellows. In 1828 Pusey took holy orders, and married shortly afterwards.

At this time his views were very much influenced by German trends in theology. However, by the end of 1833, Pusey began sympathizing with the authors of the *Tracts for the Times*. He published Tract XVIII, on fasting, at the end of 1833, adding his initials (so far the tracts had been unsigned).

When John Henry Newman converted to the Roman Catholic Church in 1841, Pusey emerged as the leader of the much-shaken Oxford Movement. But Pusey was by this time a widower, his wife having died in 1839, and much affected by personal grief. Despite this, he was extremely active in the Oxford movement (known as *Puseyism*). The effects of his sermons may be measured by the changes which were effected in their wake. For example, the practice of confession in the Church of England can be directly linked to his two sermons on *The Entire Absolution of the Penitent* in 1846, and his 1853 sermon on *The Presence of Christ in the Holy Eucharist*, which first set out the doctrine around which almost all his followers' theology later revolved, and revolutionized the practices of Anglican worship.

Development of the Oxford Movement

From the very beginning, the history of the Oxford Movement is one of controversy and squabbles about university politics which now might seem insignificant, but which were in fact crucial to the future of the Church of England. The unsuccessful attempt of the Tractarians to prevent Renn Dickson Hampden (later Bishop of Hereford), whose theology they viewed with suspicion, from becoming Regius Professor of Divinity is a case in point. The publication in 1838 of *Froude's Remains*, is another. Froude went much further than anyone else had dared before in asserting the Church of England's inherent Catholic heritage. He argued that Catholicism ought not to be confined to the Roman communion, nor Orthodoxy to the eastern churches. Perhaps the greatest explosion occurred in response to Newman's Tract Ninety, which appeared in 1841, and argued that there was nothing in the Thirty-nine Articles contrary to the Council of Trent.

In 1834, another young fellow of Oriel, Edward Pusey threw in his lot with the Tractarians. John Keble had retired from Oxford in the early 1820s moving on to the practicalities of parish work. Up until this point, the weight of leadership of the Oxford Movement had largely been borne by Newman, the Vicar of the University Church, but in the wake of the furore which accompanied Tract Ninety he increasingly withdrew to his semi-monastic establishment at Littlemore and Pusey was inevitably seen as the emerging figurehead of the movement in Oxford.

In 1843 Pusey preached a sermon before the University entitled 'The Holy Eucharist a comfort to the penitent'. Much of the sermon appealed to the Fathers and to the Caroline divines but in an increasingly politicised situation it was too much for the Evangelicals to tolerate and, despite Pusey's exhaustive explanations and massive public support, he was suspended from preaching for two years. However, no sooner had Pusey served his suspension than he was thrust into an even more prominent position by the crisis created when Newman was received into the Roman Communion in October 1845. Pusey was the only one to whom his bereft followers (who would have included Thomas Keble) could turn.

By 1845, there was a great revival of interest in liturgy and church architecture, and among its leaders was John Mason Neale, for whom the subject was very much a theological one. The Ecclesiologist, which first appeared in 1841, argued for the importance of symbol and decoration in the mysteries of worship and championed the ideas of a young Roman Catholic architect, Augustus Welby Northmore Pugin, who saw Gothic as the only proper style of Church architecture, reflecting as it did the continual religious priorities of striving for heaven through prayer, sacrament and the Christian virtues.

The strong doctrinal theology preached by the Tractarians had by now found its expression in contexts very far removed from the Universities. From the very first, the call to holiness - individual and corporate - had been at the heart of the Tractarians' teaching. It was inevitable that their attentions would turn to the social and evangelistic problems of the industrial working class. Young men who had sat at Pusey's feet found themselves called to work in new and demanding slum parishes.

The ritual innovations of which they were accused were entirely rooted in what they saw as the desperate pastoral needs they encountered. Miss Sellons's Devonport Sisters of Mercy working with the clergy of St Peter's Plymouth in the cholera epidemics of the late 1840s, for example, petitioned the parish priest, Fr George Rundle Prynne, for a celebration of the Eucharist each morning to strengthen them for their work. Thus began the first daily mass in the Church of England since the Reformation.

Similarly the clergy of St Saviour's, Leeds (a parish Pusey had endowed), laid what medicines they had on the altar at each morning's communion, before carrying them out to the many dozens of their parishioners who would die of cholera that very day. Thomas Keble's introduction of daily services in the parish of Bisley was totally in keeping with this.

The slum churches and their priests are far too many to mention, but their audacity and their piety are to be marvelled at. The Church of England at this time looked upon ritual as a wicked mimicking of the Papist Church. Vestments were an anathema to most, and yet in places such as the mission church of St George's in the East, thuribles were swung, genuflecting was encouraged and the sign of the cross was made frequently. Confessions were heard, holy anointing was practised. Here a group of priests, led by Fr Charles Lowder, carried through their interpretation of the Tractarian message. The poor must be shown the ministry of Christ not only in practical action but through the celebration of the sacraments and the preaching of the gospel. The work done by Thomas Keble in Bisley carried this into the Gloucestershire countryside where conditions were equally grim as in the cities and towns of industrialising England. In the churches he founded beauty and holiness were to be seen side by side as an antidote to the conditions in which parishioners lived and worked.

But this was not achieved without cost. It was a long and bitterly fought war in which some priests were imprisoned, many more dismissed, parish riots took place, rent-a-mob crowds were brought in, and bishops issued edicts stating areas into which they would not dare set foot. Priests such as Alexander Heriot Mackonochie were persecuted and prosecuted zealously and repeatedly for practices which are now not only acceptable but actually the norm in the Church of England - using lighted altar candles, for example.

The Oxford Movement as such was relatively short-lived although its legacy is still visible today. The rediscovered emphases on apostolic succession and the Catholicity of the church, on priesthood, on sacrament and sacrifice, on prayer, holiness and the beauty of worship, are the Tractarians' gifts to their successors. A glance round the contemporary Church of England, still vastly divergent but nevertheless teeming with colourful decorations, revised liturgies, ancient hymns, and thousands of processions, altars, oratories and retreat houses, reminds us just how dramatically the life of the English Church was renewed by the Catholic vision of those Oxford 'men of large designs'.[23]

The Sublime in Religion

The early 19th century saw massive changes in how society viewed the world.   Fading were the influences that demanded that everything should have a practical application.   Beauty, whether of nature, art or literature, and more particularly the effect of it on the soul, were starting to change how people interacted with the world.   The stark landscapes of the Derbyshire Peak District as depicted by Jane Austen in *Pride and Prejudice* are a case in point – the land that had been for generations derided for its paucity of usefulness is suddenly seen as inspirational – the experience of which will generate a sense of the sublime in the viewer. It is hardly surprising that the Tractarians who were so keen on the mystical inspiration that could be

[23] Much of this text has been taken from *What was the Oxford Movement?* on the Pusey House website – see bibliography for details

generated by ritual and beauty in worship were immersed in the Romantic movement in art and literature.

John 'Keble openly acknowledged the indebtedness of his thought and poetry to Wordsworth'.[24] However, let us not make the mistake of thinking that Tractarianism was nothing more than a fashionable trend. It would be more accurate to say that 'theology, like literature, moved from reason to feeling'.[25] The spirit of the people ached for a new and deeper meaning and Romanticism, which appeared to meet that need, permeated the thinking of the age. This was not an airy-fairy example of wishful thinking though; Bright describes the parallels between Romantic literature and the Oxford Movement as sharing 'a reverence for the past, a sense of nationalism, a preference for the natural and picturesque, a dedication to feeling as opposed to reason, aestheticism, and organicism'.[26] These are traits that exist in both the arts and theology of the 19th century.

In both the Oxford Movement and the High Church Movement which paralleled to some extent the changes in the Church of England at this time, there was a growth in the use of symbolism to express theological insights using the design of church buildings, the vestments worn by the priest and his

---

[24] Bright p385

[25] Bright p385

[26] Bright p386

acolytes and the rituals enacted during services to augment the mystical and imaginative aspects of religious experience.

The Romantics were keenly conscious of the difference between two worlds. One was the world of ideal truth, goodness, and beauty: this was eternal, infinite, and absolutely real. The other was the world of actual appearances, which to common sense was the only world, and which to the idealist was so obviously full of untruth, ignorance, evil, ugliness and wretchedness, as to compel him to dejection or indignation'[27]

This is the reasoning behind the creation of beautiful churches such as St Michael & All Angels, Bussage: that the spirits of the parishioners living in grim, poverty-ridden conditions would be somehow lifted by attendance at their parish church. The often quoted words of Wordsworth's poem *Tintern Abbey* summarise this very well:

> *A presence that disturbs me with the joy*
> *Of elevated thoughts; a sense sublime*
> *Of something far more deeply interfused,*
> *Whose dwelling is the light of setting suns,*
> *And the round ocean and the living air,*
> *And the blue sky, and in the mind of man:*
> *A motion and a spirit that impels*
> *All thinking things, all objects of all thought,*
> *And rolls through all things.*

So this is the theory behind the quiet beauty of the interior of St Michael and All Angels' Church – it is intended to generate an awe and wonder that goes

[27] Bright p387

beyond the struggles of everyday life. In other words, the building and all that goes on in it were envisioned as symbolic of the nature of God, his purity, beauty and mystery. This was, in part, a reaction or perhaps an antidote to the secularism of the 18th century on which the materialism enabled by industrialisation and prosperity had built with some success. Just as people craved emotional input from the novelists and poets, so the Oxford Movement aimed 'to rouse the Church from its lethargy and to strengthen and purify religion, by making it deeper and more real'.[28]

John Keble once wrote:

Religion is like a magic wand; once that wand touches a part of Nature, a new and heavenly light is cast upon it. Thereby we perceive that the analogies and pleasant images [of poetry] are not the meaningless sport or fancy of a clever mind, but are true evidences of Nature's voice – in truth, of Him who created Nature.[29]

Keble and his fellows saw that if they could restore a sense of mystery to the religious experience then the emphasis would change from one of instruction to one of worship; that this would require a reduction in the input of the laity during services was inevitable, the clergy and the choir would create an atmosphere in which the congregation would be drenched in awe and wonder for God. The Tractatians saw their

[28] Bright p392

[29] Bright p395

efforts as a way of expressing the paradox of Jesus the Man with Jesus the Son of God in tangible form.

Thomas Keble and the Oxford Movement

Before he arrived at Bisley, Thomas Keble is recorded as having resolved that if ever he had a parish of his own, he would at once begin daily services. Although considered something of a strange fancy at the time, as his various curates carried the practice into their subsequent parishes, it spread and has prevailed throughout the United Kingdom having previously become almost extinct. The Movement valued 17th century Anglican Divines and spiritual writings and asserted the sacred character of priestly calling and its independence from the State. It could be said that Thomas Keble was the representative of the Tractarians at Parish level; for example, he did not celebrate facing East as was the custom.

Thomas Keble published tracts under the pseudonym Richard Nelson. The first being on 4th December 1833 on the subject of Bishops, Priests and Deacons. (see Appendix 1). This was followed by *The Athanasian Creed* on 6th January 1834, *Length of the Public Service* on 21 September 1834, *Whether a Clergyman of the Church of England be now bound to have Morning and Evening Prayers daily in his Parish Church* on 24 August 1838 (with a conclusion by George Prevost) – all under the name of Richard Nelson. It should be noted that his brother John also published a tract using this pseudonym – a tract entitled *Baptism* on 25 June 1834.[30]

Thomas Keble's work in Bisley is a perfect example of how the melding of the spiritual with the wonderfull was to be achieved. He had a two-pronged attack: on one level, by instituting daily services he changed the frequency with which worship was possible while, on a totally different level, he was responsible for creating beautiful worship-spaces in which people could experience God. After all, the Tractarians argued that 'Architecture is an emblem of the invisible abstract, no less than Holy Baptism and the Lord's Supper'.[31] There is a stress on Christian Faith being the way to understand spiritual truth supported by the organs of the senses: the beauty of a building, the scent of incense, the mystery of vestments, the sound of music. All these things have a symbolic value in every element of their makeup; the buildings have a specific symbolism:

They should be cruciform and pointing eastward. The inside is divided into three parts: the nave (the ship that carries us), representing the Church Militant or the Church in this world; the chancel, separated from the nave by three steps up (the Trinity) and the cross upon the screen (death), representing the Church Expectant (the Intermediate State roughly comparable to the Roman Catholic Purgatory); and the sanctuary with the altar, representing the Church Triumphant or Heaven. In

---

[30] All these tracts are available on the internet: **https://en.wikipedia.org/wiki/Tracts_for_the_Times** .

[31] Bright p402

fact, practically all features of the church came to have symbolic value. The baptismal font, formerly placed at the front of the building so that all could see, was removed to the rear because it is by baptism that one enters the Church. The font is octagonal since eight represents eternity, the quincunx is on the altar to symbolise the five wounds of Christ, and the lectern is supported by an eagle, the sign of St John. The celebrant's vestments, their signs, and their colours all have symbolic value. The alb is purity and the stole is the yoke assumed by the priest'.[32]

To the modern eye, the buildings created by the Tractarians are 'normal' but to the churchgoers of the 19th century they would have been strange and mysterious. The people were accustomed to having the pulpit in a central position with a communion table (it was a simple wooden table by law) at which a minister in a simple, black cassock would officiate. Holy Communion was celebrated four times a year – at Christmas, Easter, Pentecost and after harvest. It is perhaps noteworthy that at Easter 1800 there were only six communicants at St Paul's Cathedral in London. The language of the liturgy had been simplified as well, removing any mystical references (e.g. Behold the Lamb of God!) and there were no hymns. It could be argued that at this period, the Church of England was in serious danger of ceasing to exist in any meaningful way. Its condition vastly more lamentable than that we know today. That it is still alive and kicking is in no small part due to the activities and enthusiasm of the members of the Oxford Movement.

[32] *Bright 402*

This Tablet is erected in grateful remembrance of two faithful ministers of the word of GOD and His holy sacraments, who by their labours and the example of their lives, served each his own generation in this Parish. The Revd. THOMAS KEBLE, B.D. sometime fellow of Corpus Christi College Oxford, Vicar, 1827-1873, and his son, The Rev. THOMAS KEBLE, M.A. sometime fellow of Magdalen College Oxford, Hon. Canon of Gloucester and Rural Dean, Vicar, 1873-1902.

Remember them that have the rule over you, who have spoken unto you the word of GOD; whose faith follow. They watch for your souls as they that must give account.

Plaque in Bisley Parish Church

Chapter 4 - St Michael and All Angels

Rev. Hayward, writing in the Parish Magazine for December 1911, quotes Rev. Robert Suckling in maintaining that the whole idea for funding the building of a church was the result of a sermon of Rev. J. H. Newman preached to a congregation of freshmen at Oxford. He took as his subject the financial assistance supplied by their families that enabled them to study at Oxford and suggested that they should reflect their gratitude by limiting 'their luxuries and even their comforts for five long years, and with the money so saved build a Church' (Hayward's words).

Thus it was that on 28th May 1839 a group of Dr Pusey's students met at Christchurch, Oxford and formed a 'Society of Sacrificial Giving'. It is highly unlikely that Dr Pusey was present at the first meeting as his wife had died a mere two days previously, though it is reasonable to assume that he fully supported the idea.

Whilst it is true that Newman, the most eloquent and gifted of the leaders of the Tractarian movement, did give such a sermon, some credit should be given to the influence of a work entitled *Rich Man's Duty* by Dr. Wells in the formation of this project. Nevertheless, it is clear that Newman was a prime mover in the formation of the group whose influence went beyond church-building in the physical sense. As Rev. Hayward reports, the Rev. Suckling's memoir (as preserved by Isaac Williams) clearly records the founding of St Michael and All Angels had much wider impact:

Hearing about this [the Society of Sacrificial Giving]*, and reading the memoirs of its first Vicar, led two noble sons of the Church to take Holy Orders, and dedicate their lives to the service of the Master – William Dalrymple Maclagan, the late Archbishop of York and the saintly Bishop Wilkinson of Truro and S. Andrews.*[33]

Plainly, there was great work afoot in the church at this time, for it was there, at that meeting of Pusey's students, that a spark was kindled that would, though the dedication of that tiny band, become a steady flame which would shed light and warmth on generations of people in the tiny hamlet known as Bussage.

The idea was a simple one. Twenty private Christians would contribute to a fund for 5 years in order to provide enough money to build a church. Each member donated £20 per annum or more as long as it was an 'inconvenience' or sacrifice for them to do so. The men set out to raise £2,000 but eventually raised £5,000, two and a half times their original goal!

The members of the group intended to remain anonymous and most have achieved that but some of them are known:

- Rev F. Menzies, a Lancashire gentleman and

---

[33] Parish Magazine December 1911

Fellow of Brazenose 1837-67, he was made deacon in 1839 and priested in1840

- Rev W. H. Ridley, who obtained his BA from Christchurch, he was made deacon in 1839 and priest in 1840 after which he became Rector of Hambledon, Bucks. (1840-82)
- Rev Isaac Williams, A Fellow of Trinity College after his BA (1826), he was curate at St Mary's Oxford (Newman's Church) and a friend of both Newman and Thomas Keble.
- Rev F. M. R. Barker, after obtaining his BA at Oriel, he was eventually ordained in 1843 there being some doubt about his health which prevented earlier ordination. He became Vicar of Sandford, and lived later at The Mansion, Bisley.
- F. H. Murray, son of the Bishop of Rochester who became rector of Chislehurst, Kent. [a note is made in the Nov 1902 edition of the parish mag of his death on 11 October.]
- Rev H. Woollcombe, who obtained his BA from Christchurch in 1835. He later became Archdeacon of Barnstaple. (Rev. Macleod was a friend of his son's)
- Rev H. Burrows – St John's College, BA 1937. He was ordained deacon in 1839.

As may be seen from this list, not all the members of the group were genuinely undergraduates at this time. Such is the power of myth!

Handwritten documents relating to the rules of the Society written in 1839 by Canon Murray were passed to Rev. Hayward in 1911 and a transcript of these is provided at Appendix II

In 1842, Rev. Isaac Williams left Oxford to come to Bisley as curate under Thomas Keble and it was here that he subsequently married and settled down. It was through this connection that the attention to the 'Oxford Twenty' was drawn to the conditions at Bussage which was one of the most forsaken parts of the Bisley parish.

The Parish Magazine for October 1897 gives an extract from the original manuscript 'application' submitted by Rev. Thomas Keble putting Bussage forward as a likely contender for the new church. Several points are highlighted in this document which show how very detailed Keble's study of the area was and how close to his heart this project became. The following specific points leap out from the application:

The size and situation of the proposed parish:
'The hamlet of Bussage is distant from Stroud 2½ miles, Bisley Church 2¼, Chalford Chapel 1, Oakridge Chapel 2½, Brimscombe Chapel 1¼ (not in the parish). The population of Bussage is 400, which with that of Eastcombe, Todesmere (*sic*), Brownshill, and Blackness, would make an amount of 900. But it is not yet determined precisely what District will be assigned to the Chapel: the probable amount of population to be provided for is 700.' Keble points out that 'although some of the distances may appear small, yet the hills are so steep that many persons are entirely prevented from going to Chalford, Bisley and Brimscombe, especially old persons, mothers of families etc.' Interestingly from a social history point

of view, he stresses that 'There is no person of wealth or influence in the hamlets' which does underline the role that such persons were expected to play in the life of the countryside.

The lamentable state of the people:
'The general character of the population is that of poor cloth manufacturers. The state of the trade is now (1842) very bad, and extreme distress prevails. "The destitution of the people it is in vain to attempt to describe" (Extract from Mr Keble's letter).'

Suitable sites:
'Several sites have been proposed, but none at present fixed: there will be no difficulty in obtaining one. They are situated in most beautiful spots, which is the character of the country immediately adjoining.'

Keble added that the church would have some financial support: 'For Endowment a sum equal to or more than £1,000 is promised: that is to say, £30 with a house, or £50 without one, may be expected.'

The application was successful and according to Lambert's history 'Keble wrote to a friend in December of that year saying that he had heard from Barker that "there is every reason to hope that a church will be built at Bussage".

It should perhaps be noted here that Bussage church was built by committed Prayer Book men who took a very anti-Roman stance, an ironic comment considering the accusations of popery later targeted at St Michael & All Angels.[34] The subject of Roman Catholicism was very much in the news in the 1850s. Not only were the Roman Catholics actively seeking parity with all other people in the UK by petitioning Queen Victoria but they were also holding meetings all around the country, trying to persuade the people of the validity of their cause. One such meeting was reported in the local paper:

Extract from the Stroud Free Press of Friday December 6th 1850:

On Tuesday evening last, a very large and influential meeting was held at the Subscription Rooms in this town, on the 'papal aggressions' and in vindication of the great principles of civil and religious liberty. The interest felt in this neighbourhood in the movement now in progress on the Romish question, and in the general subject of the liberty of the people, may be judged of from the fact that notwithstanding the charge for admission, nearly 1,500 people were assembled, the large room together with the gallery and platform, being literally crowded.

The article goes on to list the names of many clergy who attended this meeting but it is perhaps notable that none from the Bisley parish are shown. Was their apparent High Church stance perhaps too controversial? After all, when the church at Bussage was first mooted, it even looked, briefly, as if it would be supported by a small convent. Dr Pusey wanted to establish communities of nuns under the

[34] see the section on Revs. Macleod and Hayward in Chapter 6 for details.

auspices of the Church of England and at one time he had thought to site one at Bisley. As it happened, Isaac Williams had a house at Bussage at the bottom of the steep hill and one lady – a Mrs Foljambe - came to inspect the property. However, the fact that, at that time, the church in Bussage had not yet been built was an insurmountable obstacle from her point of view and she but refused to do anything more until the church was built so the idea came to nothing.

Choosing the Site and Building the Church

According to Mary Rudd, the Oxford Twenty determined that the church they built 'should be substantial, beautiful and handsomely adorned, in a place to be decided on when the funds allowed'.[35] What the founders had not counted on was having to deal with geological problems; the land around Bussage is decidedly unstable consisting of a wide band of what is called 'foundered strata' which is subject to landslip.

The January 1897 edition of the Parish Magazine underlines the ongoing instability of the landscape: Thursday, 17 December – Rev Macleod wrote to The Times: *'I was roused from sleep by a rumbling noise and felt ten or twelve distinct vibrations, which were followed an instant or so later by a quivering of the earth. The movement seemed to travel from north-west or west-north-west to south-west … and the china etc in the room was much disturbed. As the*

[35] Rudd p345

movement passed away, the dog chained in my stable yard barked violently. A lady living about five-eighths of a mile south gives the hour of the shock as about 5.40. At Stroud ... it was felt stronger. Earthquakes have been known here previously, though none as severe are remembered.' At the Communion held on that day, and on the following Sunday, 'thanks were offered to God for deliverance from peril and danger'

'The first site chosen for the erection of the Church was below the field leading from Bussage to the House of Mercy [in Brownshill], now a garden; but this was abandoned as being too near the line of occasional landslips. The existence of several yew trees ... below Bussage House, decided the founders to select that most beautiful but somewhat inconvenient spot. There the foundation was laid on 21 November 1844.'[36] According to a letter from Sister Mary Augustine (daughter of Rev. Robert Suckling) it was the old yew-tree on the site which decided their choice of a site.

But even then their troubles were not over, 'the site chosen proving to be not quite as stable as desired, the foundations of the north wall were strengthened by oak piles, driven into the hill-side. The Church, as first built, consisted of a Chancel with vestry, nave, and tower at the west end and South porch, in the style of the Decorated period. The bays of the arch-braced roof of the nave are supported by demi-figures of angels with hands folded in prayer.'[37]

[36] Rudd p 345

The Ecclesiologist had nothing but praise for the new church. Not only was the altar of the approved Tractarian pattern - a slab of Purbeck marble standing on six legs – but the chancel was paved with the equally approved caustic tiles and the sill of the south window lowered to provide a sedilia – a feature which the Ecclesiologist noted with great approval. The sacristy was correctly placed on the north side of the chancel and a low oak screen divided the chancel from the nave. The stall benches were returned, so that prayers could be read from the eastward position and an oak lectern was also provided.

The church is strikingly situated in a narrow valley of the Cotswold Hills, among a cluster of mountain cottages, far apart from any other church. At its west end stands a yew-tree, which determined the position of the church.[38]

This description makes the site of the church sound very romantic though one has to question how this relates to everyday, practical usage for the occupants of the 'mountain' (!) cottages.

The architect tasked with designing the building was J P Harrison; he was a supporter of the old style of wooden roof. A local builder with an international reputation – Solomon Wallis – was responsible for constructing the church; he and his sons, Samuel and William, Thomas, had a hand in many churches

37 Rudd p 346

[38] Malcolm Lambert quoting the Ecclesiologist article

including the Crimean Memorial Church raised in Constantinople, the American Church in Paris, the new Law Courts in the Strand and the Imperial Institute, Kensington, as well as the Queen Victoria Memorial at Buckingham Palace and the Naval College at Dartmouth. The family were active in the Bussage parish, holding positions of Churchwardens for many years. Another son, Edward, left the Wallis Bequest to the church. I daresay they were not enthralled by the fact that Keble was determined that the tower should be strong enough to take a spire.

The Church bell was cast at the famous Whitechapel foundry in London.

As is invariably the case as generation succeeds generation, the much admired arrangements did not meet with the approval of Ritualists of later generations. The altar was subsequently deemed to be too low, and too small and it was enlarged during the incumbency of Rev. Christopher Smyth by the addition of a longer stone slab and gradine and tabernacle. The low screen was built up with Rood, and the stalls in the chancel were turned to face north and south in order to accommodate a surpliced choir.

After a considerable amount of pleading and nagging by Rev. Macleod, the Stations of the Cross were purchased and installed, though it took over two years to raise sufficient funds to do this. The August 1897 edition of the Parish Magazine contained one of many appeals to the parishioners in response to a special offer from Mayer & Co (makers of the Stations) who were relocating and trying to offload stock. They were offering the remaining four Stations at a reduced price of £3 10s each. Rev. Macleod appealed for funds to secure them and the October edition reported that the Vicar and Wardens had decided to accept this offer even though they did not have the cash at that time. The full set was only completed in December 1897.

Other alterations include a reredos originally painted by Mr Leslie and repainted by his daughter in 1923. The chancel screen incorporating a plain cross was presented to the church by Rev. Arnott which, after the First World War 'was enriched with a cresting, over which the Rood was placed'.[39]

Church plate comprising a silver-gilt chalice and paten, a small silver chalice and paten for sick communions, a silver-gilt flagon, alms dish and candlesticks had been presented to the church by the founders. The first incumbent, Rev. Robert Suckling, added a pair of cruets and his son, also Rev. Robert Suckling who held the living of St. Alban's, Holborn and maintained a strong link with the parish for many years, donated a further set 'in memory of his brother Lionel, baptised at Bussage'[40]. A Sanctuary lamp was given in memory of Rev. Suckling junior.

But the church was not to be an edifice in isolation, more was required in order to set up the parish: a house for the clergy to live in and, most importantly

[39] Johnson p10

[40] ibid

71

of all, a financial endowment to pay for a clergyman. Keble notes that: 'For Endowment a sum equal to or more than £1000 is promised: that is to say, £30 with a house, or £50 without one, may be expected.' He also knew how desperately a school was required and his plan included the provision of such a necessity.

'The need for further room in order to seat the inmates of the Bussage House of Mercy later led to the addition of a south aisle opening into the nave by an arcade of three bays, designed by Bodley'.[41]

Thomas Keble laid the foundation stone of the new church on 21st November 1844 and although the actual site of the original stone is not known, Keble took a rubbing of the inscription on it:

In Honorem Dei.
Mortuorum et vivorum Domini
Et in curam pauperum in Christo,
Haec Ecclesia fundata est Cal XI Dec.
A.S.MDCCCXLIV
Suis impensis oedificant viginiti
Academiae Oxoniensis alumni
Ignoti quidem his locis sed Dei noti

This translates as:
To the Honour of God
The Lord both of the dead and the living
And in pious care for the poor in Christ,
The Foundation Stone of this Church is laid on the
21s day of November,
in the Year of Salvation 1844.

[41] Rudd p 346

Built at the sole expense of twenty
Scholars of the University of Oxford
Unknown in this place, but known to God

An entry in an old diary discovered in the summer of 1901 reveals that 'building commenced on November 21st 1844, and a supper was given to the men at William Alley's (now the Post Office) the same evening.' However, as Rev. Macleod notes in the Parish Magazine in July 1901 'it must have been a long trial of patience to them [the founders]' pointing out that, although their original meeting had been held in 1839, the church not ready to be consecrated until 1846.

As far as accommodation for the incumbent went, 'Mr Suckling lived for a time at Brownshill House'[42] 'Miss A. M. Suckling states in a note on Brownshill House, that it was a cottage added on to by a Mr Wynn in the reign of William IV. ... Mr Wynn's son sold it to a Mr Gardiner, a wealthy man, who sold it in his turn to the Rev. Richard Champernowne (son-in-law of the Rev. Thomas Keble, senior) for a Parsonage for Bussage. However the house proved to be inconveniently distant from the Church, school and village.'[43]

Consecration

The church was consecrated by Bishop Monk of

[42] Johnson p 11

[43] Rudd P354

Gloucester amidst a great Tractarian demonstration of the Faith on 6th October 1846. Forty-four robed clergy were in attendance and Rev W. H. Ridley (one of the Twenty) preached, choosing as his text Zechariah Ch 4 v10.[44] The clergy robed at The Ram and processed to the site of the church to hear the sermon, after which the 'procession re-formed and marched round the Churchyard, which the Bishop then consecrated.'[45]

Ridley's sermon was entitled: 'The Day of Small Things' and, from the excerpt Miss Johnson records in an appendix to her history, it is clear that the enthusiasm and energy that caused the church to be created in the first place had in no way abated.

Is it not 'a day of small things' when we meet to offer to God this sacred building, in itself small, raised by the efforts of a few, who have given, some of their abundance, others of their poverty, to the honour of GOD? ... what then, was that day when the thought to undertake this work was first breathed in secret between two or three friends, unknown in this place, in an upper chamber in a distant city? And their work is now accomplished, and they are permitted to behold its accomplishment! ... Remember those who have been permitted to be the honoured instruments of building this house ... pray for them, that they may 'do greater works than these' in self-discipline, and works of faith and love; and if GOD will, in outward works for the Church. ... And if there be one here

---

[44] Parish Magazine August 1901

[45] Johnson p7

present who, seeing how GOD accepteth a small offering, feels his heart warmed with gratitude and zeal, let him in this blessed Feast praise GOD with thanksgiving, let him there ask for grace himself to do great things.

The first interment to take place in the new churchyard was that of Samuel Bingle, who had been killed by Sam Seville's horse at Toadsmoor. His funeral took place on 4th April 1847. However, until the legal separation of Bussage from the parish of Bisley had been sanctioned by law, it was necessary for any Baptisms or Burials to be entered in the Register Books for the Mother Church of Bisley, which accounts for the Burial of Samuel Bingle not being found in the Parish Register where the first interment recorded is that of Ann Drew, which took place on August 27, 1848. The first entry of Baptisms occurs under the same date, and the earliest recorded Marriage took place on 16th July 1849.

The Creation of the Parish

The parish was legally constituted in 1848 by an Order in Council dated 29th August 1848. Held by Queen Victoria at Osborne House, the Council defined the boundaries of the new 'Chapelry District of Bussage' and assigned a small portion of the tything – omitting Eastcombe and Brownshill. The actual designation states:

The Chapelry District of Bussage is bounded on the north-west and west by the parish of Stroud: on the south and south-east by the Chalford District as far as the north-west corner of Frith Wood; and on the east and north-east by the remaining part of the parish of Bisley from which it is separated by a line drawn in a northerly direction from the said north-west corner of Frith Wood, across Bisley Common to the footpath leading from the said Common to Daniel's Farm, along which said footpath the boundary line then proceeds north-easterly up the middle of the latter footpath, as far as Cuckoo Lane; and then proceeds north-westerly, westerly and again north-westerly, up the middle of that lane and crossing Bismore Bridge, meets the boundary of the before-mentioned parish of Stroud.' (Johnson Appendix III)

Chapter 5 - Reverend Robert Suckling   1818 - 1843

Robert Alfred Suckling was the eldest son and heir to the property of the ancient family of that name, of Woodton, in the County of Norfolk. He was related to the mother of Lord Nelson, and her brother, Captain Suckling, was the professional tutor and early patron of the great Admiral. Sir John Suckling, the Poet; his father, of the same name, had been Comptroller of the Household and Privy Counsellor to King James and King Charles the First.

Young Robert's initial choice of career was not the church and in 1831, at the age of thirteen, he entered the Navy.   Whilst his career was extremely successful, two near death bouts of yellow fever while off the coast of Africa, gave him to think about the purpose of his life and, in 1839, he left the Navy and determined to dedicate his life to God's work. In the same year, he cut himself off from his inheritance by consenting to the ending of the entail.

Extract from Suckling's private journal, 1837
"We arrived at Sierra Leone in the beginning of December. We were boarded by a boat in the entrance of the river, advising us not to go in, as the fever was raging, and some of the vessels that we must necessarily anchor near, had lost crews. We anchored. I never knew what heat was before ; it is dreadfully hot.

We have been ten days out, and are not 100 miles from Sierra Leone. We have five cases of fever, now pronounced to be the yellow fever, and very bad; we entertained hopes that it was otherwise. It will no doubt run through the ship; so it has hitherto. We have new cases every day, and we are preparing now for sickness.   Poor is dead; he died raving mad; we have buried him.

Jan. 20th, 1838. I have had the fever, and am now convalescent. What has not passed in the short time elapsed since I was taken ill? I have been at death's door, and calmly said to myself, death is approaching. It had no horrors for me: I felt not that I could have no hope. It appears to me a dream; I cannot imagine how I could have been so indifferent, so hardened; but I find it is the nature of the disease: all are so. We are on our way to the Island of Ascension. The ship is a perfect pest-house; our decks are covered with the sick; we have only five men well. We are becalmed on the Line; it is horrible; nothing but the groans of the sick and the ravings of the dying are to be heard. I have been in this state. I do not feel thankful that I am preserved; I ought to do so, and I strive. There is nobody to offer a word of encouragement; all are alike indifferent. The name of our Saviour is never heard excepting in blasphemy. I must go back to the time of my being taken ill: — it was in the middle watch; I had relieved the second Lieutenant about one. I felt rather cold, and put on warmer clothing. I was walking the deck with a light heart, for I had no cares. A breeze had just sprung up; we were proceeding to our destination (Dix Cove on the Gold Coast) and I was picturing to myself what it was like, for all was perfectly new to me. I felt a sudden pain shoot down my back, so violent, that I leant against the ship's side for support. Upon attempting to rise, I found a pain in all my joints. I had the day before seen a man at the wheel seized in a similar manner; I had therefore no doubt but that it was the fever, and leaving the orders with S, I went down to my hammock, asking him to tell M, the assistant-surgeon, when he went his rounds, to come and see me : this was about two o'clock. What an age it seemed till four, when the doctor came! He came at last; how glad I was to see him! I gradually grew better. Two men who had left the Orestes with me came to see me, and I well recollect one of them saying: "He will never see England again".   I thought so too. I remained ill more than a week, and was then permitted to get up a short time every day. All my inquiries about the sick were evaded. I at last found that poor Saunders and twelve men had died, and seventy were ill in their hammocks. I came on deck every day now I was quite accustomed to the groans of the sick, and day by day I saw the dead brought up until we had numbered eight and twenty."

On the 22nd of April, in the year 1840, he married Anna Maria, the daughter of Dr Yelloly of Cavendish Hall, Suffolk; and in the following June entered Caius College, Cambridge. However, during his undergraduate career his time and thoughts were much taken up with his all-consuming religious faith and as the end of his studies approached he wrote to his wife:

I so wish the examination was over, it takes up all my thoughts; I have no time for anything such as I would wish to pursue. I am ashamed to be obliged to lay aside my daily study of the Bible; and everything I think or do must be to other points. I wish this was over, and the time come when my whole and undivided attention may be given up to the study of God's Word and His Will.

Clearly he was looking towards the Church though his hopes were dashed when he was refused Ordination by the then Bishop of Ely. However, he persisted and his determination was rewarded; in September 1843, he was ordained Deacon at Gloucester.

His first parish experience was as curate at Kemerton where he worked from 1843 to 1846. As Isaac Williams comments in his memoir of Suckling, 'The two or three years after Ordination usually give the whole complexion to a clergyman's after life.'

And it may be fairly said that the combination of Suckling's innate self-denial, personal energy and application to duty flowered under the benign and generous influence of Archdeacon Thorp, his Rector at Kemerton, enabling Suckling to convert his personal faith into practical action in his work in the parish, a training that would stand him in very good stead when he later moved to Bussage.

A parishioner from Kemerton, who had been asked to describe Suckling at this time, wrote of him:

Mr. Suckling's division of his time in this first year was, I believe, the early part of the morning to the school, the afternoon to the parish, and the evening to study. He urged the habit of private prayer in Churches strongly, and especially at that season [Lent]; the Church had been first left open for the workmen; he began the custom of leaving it constantly so, and it has never since been discontinued, nor have I ever heard of any inconvenience arising from it. The bell-ringers now passed through the Church, and to awaken in them a higher sense of their office was another object of his endeavours, and with much success. After a time, they of their own accord drew up rules for their conduct, which they submitted to his approbation. On the entrance of Lent, he had a request from the parish clerk, a mason, to remove the evening service to an hour late enough to enable him and some others to attend after work.

As was afterwards frequently commented upon, Suckling had a particular concern and sympathy for people as individuals, refusing to consider a family collectively as an entity or, even as was customary at this time, as a patriarchy, but treating every member of that family as the object of his concern and care, taking an interest in what each one was doing. This trait continued throughout his all-too-brief ministry.

Bussage

Despite a bout of illness, in 1846 Robert Suckling was offered and accepted the charge of the new church that had been built at Bussage, near Bisley. As he wrote in his journal: "By the blessing of God, my health being much restored, left Mudiford for Bisley, July 29th, 1846."

He quickly set to work in the new parish of St Michael and All Angels, putting his newly-acquired skills to good use in building up the parish from nothing: organising the church and services, starting a choir, overseeing the local dispensary and workhouse, and later on assisting in the foundation of the House of Mercy. All this he attacked with a realistic and practical faith. His influence was far-reaching - a fact that only dawned on Suckling slowly and, once realised, caused him considerable alarm and apprehension because of the responsibility he felt it laid on his shoulders – consequently he felt deeply responsible and anxious that the impact of his work should be positive and this clearly put a lot of strain on him, a burden he shouldered only through his reliance on prayer.

It was during this period that Isaac Williams met Robert Suckling and it is perhaps worthy of note that he says the following of the young priest: 'There was something in his natural character that would have reminded a stranger of his great relative.' He is, of course, referring to Horatio Nelson, and goes on to quote what 'the poet says of Nelson,

To him, e'en like the burning Levin,
Short, bright, resistless course was given.'

Whilst there is something of the Victorian romantic in these lines, they do paint a definite picture of a man who is charismatic and burning with both the desire and the ability to make a difference to the people in his parish.

Walking through the woods in a January fog on your way to work long hours at the mill cannot have been very pleasant

The following extract from a letter Suckling wrote to a friend describes graphically the conditions amongst which he was working and the obligation he keenly felt to improve the lives of his parishioners:

My lot is fixed here; here I must run the days of my pilgrimage; and I cannot but be thankful that I am placed where there are no good things of the world to tempt or to ensnare me, and where, by God's

grace, the suffering and hard bondage that is around me must keep me from living a life of self-indulgence and ease. My poor parishioners mostly work at the mills; and your heart would bleed were you to see the children, from eleven upwards, many of them of weak and delicate frames, who have to toil to enrich others. These poor things have to leave here at half-past five in the morning in all weathers, and do not return till seven at night; there must be fifty or sixty of them here. The only time I can see them is Saturday afternoon, when they leave work at four, or the Sunday; and then it cheers my heart to see their cheerful faces: they seem to enjoy this day of rest.

He was indefatigable in working for the benefit of the parish, setting up and running late evening Bible study/exposition classes for the workers; Holy Communion on the evening of the Ascension, All Saints' and Maundy Thursday, and a Midnight Communion service on New Year's Eve which caused raised eyebrows!

It was the custom with Thomas Keble and his curates to be in church some time before service and Suckling was no exception, using this time to intercede for those of his flock who did attend church, and also for those who did not. During the week there was daily Morning and Evening Prayer and on Sundays he held services at 10, 3, and 6 with sermon. He was determined to take the church's work to the poorest and most neglected parts of the country and with so many of his parishioners working long hours and living in abject poverty, he had plenty of opportunity to do this in Bussage and

Brownshill.

Williams cites an example of the effectiveness of Suckling's work as a parish priest. "A woman had a little boy killed at a mill: she was asked if she had seen Mr. Suckling. "Yes," she replied, "I sent for him at once; I felt as if I knew not how to bear it till he came."

There are many instances quoted in Williams' memoir that demonstrate Suckling's unerring ability to see value in an individual.

I remember an old lunatic woman who used to sit basking in the sun, and noticed those who passed with vacant stare and half-incoherent murmurings; most persons would have had no other feeling than that of indifference towards such an object; but he once mentioned her to me and dwelt on some striking and impressive saying she had made use of to him on the importance of eternity ... I never looked on that woman again as I had done before. Thus would he draw out from each, however humble, what they had within of heaven.

Williams goes on to report that a friend once commented that: "it was more easy to be religious in conversation and action in his [Suckling's] house than in any other. On my first visit it was just upon twelve o'clock he gently asked me if I would join with him in his usual prayer for that hour from Bishop Cosin's Devotions."

Robert Suckling was not only liberal with his time

but also with the limited money and items at his disposal: he subscribed to the fund for building Perth Cathedral, and among the offerings he made were several articles of plate, with two crests upon them. A friend hinted to Williams that these items probably constituted the last articles of any value that Suckling possessed of his heritage.

Early drawing of Bussage Church featured in the book A short memoir of the Rev. Robert Alfred Suckling by Isaac Williams. Publication date 1853

However, despite the image thus presented of an energetic and enthusiastic priest going about his work, the fact remains that Suckling was regularly laid low by illness. This ailment, probably the result of the yellow fever that nearly killed him, recurred regularly. Even today, yellow fever is not curable and like malaria, returns periodically causing fever, sickness, muscle pain, and in more serious attacks it can cause jaundice or bleeding from the mouth, nose or eyes. This would not have made his task any easier. Indeed he writes to a friend in 1847 that:

'Though I got your letter on Sunday I have been too poorly to look into it till now. I was scarcely able to get through the morning service, and unable to attend the afternoon, but I hope to go to-night; had it not been thus with me, I should not have delayed sending an answer so long.' Even in sickness, he drove himself to perform his duties.

The year after settling at Bussage, Suckling went on a trip to Madeira with Archdeacon Thorp, partly it seems for his health and partly to consider the state of the Church of England there. He wrote to his wife:

Madeira, March 12th 1847
But the worst of all is the famine – really and truly a famine – no bread to be had in the Island for money. ... They are daily expecting food which has been sent for; but till that comes, the state of the poor is ... dreadful. ... I have today been in a house where two hundred and fifty houseless persons are collected from the streets, and furnished with straw and one meal a day, by order of the Governor.

Madeira, April 8th
I certainly am much stronger, and walk about and laugh at such hills as the little hills at Bussage, but the great distress that has prevailed here has been enough to prevent one's getting better ; some people have died, but thank God, it is over now to a great extent,— i. e., provisions are cheaper. Since I last wrote, we have been worse than before ; the provisions I mentioned were consumed, and starvation appeared again : you could not walk

anywhere without being met by starving people, begging in the most piteous manner ; mothers, with children like death, pointing to their breasts, to show they had no milk ; five hundred beggars were gathered into a confiscated convent, and there fed upon vegetable broth, once a day, which it is considered is all that one third of the whole population have.

The impact of Robert Suckling's work in Bussage is perhaps best shown in the results of a religious census carried out in 1851.

The numbers estimated to attend services following the church opening were 100 in the morning, 150 in the afternoon, and 200 in the evening, with a further 80 scholars attending each of the two Sunday school classes. The vicar completing the return was Robert A Suckling, a man whose opinions and practices were said at this time to be of the 'highest Tractarian theories'. He worked tirelessly with the poor of his parish and was 'instrumental in making a remarkable change in the population and in establishing a House of Refuge for female penitents'.

However, towards the end of Suckling's life it appears that '*During these labours of love a change appears to have come over his views, some alienation in feelings and sympathies between him and the party to which he had been attached took place*'[46]. There is little evidence for this remaining but the Reverend Isaac Williams was moved to question something Suckling said: '*We do not think*

[46] Peter Drover's text

that any Tractarian would have expressed himself in terms like these.'[47] Could the practical, everyday challenges of parish life perhaps have battered at the corners of the high-minded expectations of the still relatively young priest?

We can only guess at his thoughts at this time although we do have his words, his prayers, which give some idea of where he stood with regard to both his own personal faith and the Tractarian movement itself.

His prayers

Great and glorious God, Who art of purer eyes than to behold iniquity; I cannot speak to Thee, for I am vile! Yet Thou hast commanded me to draw near to Thy throne of grace, through the merits and mediation of Thy well-beloved Son. For His sake, I beseech Thee, put forth Thine hand and touch my mouth, and take away mine iniquity, and purge my sin.

O Lord, Thou hast called me to be a watchman and a shepherd over a portion of that flock which Thou hast purchased with Thy Blood; who is sufficient for these things? That my sufficiency may be of Thee, Who dost make Thy strength perfect in Thy servant's weakness. Give me, I beseech Thee, the tongue of the learned, that I may know how to speak a word in season to him that is weary, and to warn the

---

[47] Peter Drover's text

rebellious. Open my understanding, that I may understand the Scriptures; talk with me in all my goings out and comings in, and make my heart to burn within me. When I speak the word of life to Thy people, make it in me as a burning fire; and do Thou open their hearts to attend to the things that may be spoken. Let Thy Word, Lord, ever be glorified.

Pour out Thy Holy Spirit abundantly on me, that I may give myself continually to prayer, and the ministry of the Word; give me the wisdom of the serpent, and the harmlessness of the dove; make me instant in season and out of season; let my loins be ever girded about, and my light burning.

Fill me with such an ardent love for the souls of men, that I count not my life dear unto me, but be ready to die for the Name of the Lord Jesus. Shed abroad Thy love so abundantly in my heart, that I may answer, 1 Lord, Thou knowest all things, — Thou knowest that I love Thee.

Strengthen me in the inner man with the power of Thy might, that I may pull down all the strongholds of Satan; give me grace to sow seeds of righteousness, in the morning going forth to sow, and in the evening withholding not the hand. And do Thou, O gracious God, give the increase, that I labour not in vain; but, if it be Thy will, may see the trees of righteousness bud and bring forth fruit abundantly, that our children may grow up as the polished corners of the temple.

His Death

Robert Suckling died on All Saints' Day, 1851; like the Lord he served so well, he was aged only 33. On the day he died, he celebrated the Holy Communion in the morning and it has been suggested that during the last few weeks of his life he seemed to be preparing for the end, as if he knew it was coming; he spent, we are told, hours daily in intercession for his little flock, whose every trial was his care. His heart was set upon them. And he was laid amidst that flock in the churchyard on the lovely slope of the Gloucestershire hills. A vignette of the church engraved by Willmore is on the title-page of Mr. Williams' memoir.

Such is his professional legacy. His personal legacy may be read in the actions of his children. His son Robert went into the church and, as has been mentioned several times herein, he kept his links with Bussage throughout his life. The younger son, Lionel, features in the following item from the Parish Magazine. One feels that his father would have approved of his conduct.

Item from October 1901 Parish Magazine – *in Quirindi, New South Wales. - Mr Lionel Suckling, youngest son, 'on the evening of August 8th, at Quirindi, a large balcony, on which some 150 persons were collected, suddenly collapsed, and the whole of its occupants hurled to the ground amongst its ruins. "Mr Suckling" we quote from a local newspaper, "exhibited the qualities of a hero. With both legs broken above the ankles, he got upon his* *knees and used his arms to hold up a great section of the roofing, so as to prevent its falling on some helpless ladies and gentlemen who were round about him. Mrs Suckling, who had sustained a broken ankle, sat near him all the while, and made no complaint. She seemed more anxious about others than herself."*

Chapter 6 – Subsequent Clergy

The church had been very well set up physically by the founders who had been keen that it should not comprise the cheapest options. The result was a beautiful, well-built edifice. However, they appear not to have given much thought to the stipend and, as a result, Bussage offered a poor living to any priest taking the role of Perpetual Curate. This, in turn, had an effect on the clergy who served there as only those with private means or another source of income, who were able to use their own resources to support themselves, were able to stay for any substantial period. This situation would be complicated further for any incumbent who had a family to support, of course. One side-effect of this appears to have been that the parish attracted an unusually large number of highly-qualified priests who had either previously been missionaries, most likely accustomed to poor living conditions, who saw the parish as an extension of this work or priests who were starting out on their careers in the church and invariably ended up in high office.

However, St Michael and All Angels was not the only church in the area to attract zealous missionary priests as a plaque in the church of St John the Baptist, France Lynch shows (see photo). The Reverend Walter Lyon, originally curate at Bisley under Keble and later the first vicar of France Lynch, worked for five years with a mission in Canada. There, ironically enough, on St John the Baptist's day in 1898, he drowned in Lake La Barge whilst on his way to found a Church of England mission at

Klondike. He was 39 years old.

Plaque commemorating Rev. Walter Lyon's death

Crockfords, the Clergy directory, reports on the annual income of the living as follows;

- 1885/6 (Rev. I K Anderson) – Glebe land paid £34, Queen Anne's Bounty[48] provided £28, Ecclesiastical Commission supplied £30, making a gross income of £92 plus the house. The population of the parish at the time was 362 souls. (The average working man's wages at this time would be around £75 p.a.)
- By 1929, when Rev. Barchard was incumbent, the income was as follows: no figure is shown for glebe land, although Queen Anne's Bounty had increased to £52, Ecclesiastical Commission paid

[48] A fund formed by Queen Anne in 1704 to be used to increase the income of livings yielding less than £80 a year. It was not paid directly to incumbents, but instead was used to purchase land (generally £200-worth) income from which would then augment the living. Initially, the livings to be augmented were selected by lot from those with an annual income less than £10. Parishes worth less than £20 a year were included in the ballot in 1747, those worth less than £30 a year in 1788, by1810 the qualifying figure had risen to £50. In 1948 the administrators of the fund were replaced by the Church Commissioners for England

£135, Fees provided £2, e.o. [*Author's Note: I have not been able to discover what this abbreviation means*] - £40 – giving a gross figure of £229 (net £219) and house. The population of the parish, which had risen to 382 in 1891, had fallen again and was then 350. (The average working man's wages would be between £178 and £220 p.a. depending on his skill levels)

- In 1944, when Rev. Abell was instituted, the income was made up as follows: Queen Anne's Bounty £49, Ecclesiastical Commission £235, fees £2, e.o. £13; giving a gross figure of £299. The population had then dropped to 326.

Rev. Thomas Keble, (Junior): 1851 – 1852

Thomas was the son of Rev. Thomas Keble, Rector of Bisley. He attended Magdalen College, Oxford, was ordained deacon in 1849 and priested the following year.

He married Cornelia Sarah Cornish in 1851 but she died in 1858 and four years later, in 1862, he married Mary Caroline Turner. His four sons all became priests and he also had six daughters. Thomas Junior held several curacies, including that of Bussage after Robert Suckling's death and in 1873 he accepted the living of Bisley, succeeding his father who died two years later in 1875.

He remained as Vicar of Bisley for 30 years. In 1901 he was responsible for building the corrugated iron church in Eastcombe. His own four sons were all later ordained.

Thomas Junior's funeral took place on the 7th Jan 1903.

The coffin was covered with a purple pall bearing a large crimson cross which had previously been used for John Keble's funeral at Hursley in March 1866. His brother George conducted the funeral assisted by his sons, Thomas and Richard.

Rev. Robert George Swayne: 1852-59

Rev R G Swayne, only son of Robert Swayne of St Paul's Bristol, Gent. Oxford BA 1842, MA 1844. Deacon 1844 and Priest 1845. In 1851, aged 29, he became Curate at Tidenham, going on to become Perpetual Curate of Bussage the following year. After leaving Bussage in 1859 he became Temporary Curate of St Mary's Reading (1861).), Vicar of St Edmunds Church, Salisbury, Prebendary of Gillingham Major in Sarum Cathedral and subsequently Canon and Chancellor of that Cathedral. He died in Poole on 22nd April 1901.

During his time at Bussage, the south aisle was completed by Bodley to serve the needs of the residents of the House of Mercy.

Unfortunately, Rev R.G. Swayne, one of Keble's team, left Bussage under a cloud of episcopal displeasure.

The Bishop of Gloucester, James Henry Monk (1830-36) was tolerant of the High Churchmanship which prevailed among so many of his clergy. However in 1856, Bishop Charles Baring succeeded Monk as Bishop of Gloucester and he was a staunch evangelical. His antipathy towards the High Church movement caused problems between him and the Bisley parish. In fact, his treatment of Keble and Swayne caused W. J. Copeland, a well- known Tractarian, to write on 18th Oct 1859:

All at Bisley seems sadly upset and so will it be elsewhere. To see a man such as we know Thomas Keble to be, so treated by a State Bishop, does indeed more than ever sicken me, of the State appointments and the State interference. I do not know of anything that has left me so sad as the Bussage case. Knowing what we do of Thomas Keble, his deep seriousness and excessive sensitiveness, certainly as you and I have always felt, one of the most remarkable men we have known at all, what can one think of the hard and most unfeeling treatment he has received from one in every way his inferior. [49]

It seems the trouble had most to do with the House of Mercy. Up to 1844 there had been no mention of 'Sisters' although Mrs Poole was described as Lady Superior. It is thought that Swayne may have attempted to have the sisters professed – something which would have incensed the Bishop. Thankfully in 1861 Baring was translated to Durham and confidence was restored when his successor, William Thompson, appointed Rev. George Prevost as Archdeacon of Gloucester.

Before he moved on, Swayne left his mark on the village, as Mary Rudd states in her history: *Note on Bussage Parsonage from a Memorandum by Miss A M Suckling*
In this it is stated that in 1848 a little house on the site of the present vicarage was established as a Parsonage. About 1849 some additional rooms were built on and that new part is now the old part of the present Vicarage. The Rev. R G Swayne during his incumbency pulled down the original little house and built the Vicarage as it is now.

---

[49] Torode p 76

Rev. William Maunder Hitchcock: 1859-61

Made deacon in 1958 at Canterbury and subsequently priested 1859 in Gloucester & Bristol, he became an honorary canon of Durham (1868), and Rural Dean of Wearmouth (1880-81). Rev Hitchcock fell out with Keble over changes. Hitchcock had also moved away from the Prayer Book.

On a happier note, there is a notice in the Guardian for January 4th 1860 announcing the birth of his son in Bussage.

Rev. Alexander Poole: 1861

Rev. Alexander Poole was in post for an extremely short time as he went as canon to Bristol only months after his arrival in Bussage.

He was Canon at St Peter's Clifton from 1862-68.

There is a mention of Poole's death in the May 1899 edition of the Parish magazine· *'Rev. Alexander Poole, Rector of West Meon, and Honorary Canon of Winchester. In 1861 Mr Poole was appointed Curate-in-Charge of Bussage, but his stay here was brief, as in a few months' time he was appointed Minor Canon of Bristol Cathedral, which position he held for seven years.'*

Rev. Edmund Nelson Dean 1861-78

Rev. Dean died in Bussage on the 24 September 1878 and is buried in the churchyard of St Michael's.

In connection with the anniversary of the church's dedication, the October 1896 parish magazine mentions him with affection, commenting that it would be impossible That 'Edmund Nelson Dean, whose last earthly resting-place is beneath its walls, has forgotten it.'

His wife, Mrs Dean, founded the Guild of St Michael & All Angels in Bussage, an organisation of Christian women who met regularly. In 1874, during

Dean's incumbency, the **Rev. Edward Male** 'acted as Assistant Curate. Mr Male was here a very short time, and apparently the only visible record that remains is a single entry in the Register of Baptisms. He passed away at Oxford at the age of 79' (Excerpt from Parish Mag. March 1897).

Rev. John Smith: 1878-81

Smith was made Deacon in 1875, and priest 1876. He is shown as living in Semaphore, South Australia in the 1887 edition of Crockford's directory so obviously moved there shortly after leaving Bussage.

Robert Clissold who was Parish Clerk for many years, is recorded as saying in the Parish Magazine on the occasion of his resignation in 1900 that: *'In the Rev. J. Smith's time the services were very Low Church and the Church was never open on Week-days. There was nothing but Sunday Services.'*

Rev. Henry Arnott: 1881-85

Born 6 December 1842, son of James Moncrieff Arnott, professor of surgery at King's College, London, and twice President of the Royal College of Surgeons, Henry Arnott was educated at University College School and at University College, London.

Henry Arnott had long been interested in the work of the Church and in October 1864 had helped to found a Brotherhood of St Luke with Reginald Eager, John

Wickham Legg, Charles Frederick Lethbridge, and George William Rigden, who were all, like himself, medical students. On 2 November 1864 Robert Brett was chosen provost and Henry Arnott master of the brotherhood, which subsequently became well-known as the Guild of St Luke.

Arnott became a Fellow of the Royal College of Surgeons in 1868. From 1866 to 1869 he was surgical registrar and superintendent of post-mortems at the Middlesex Hospital and was elected assistant surgeon in 1870.

Arnott lived at Beckenham whilst he was working at St Thomas's. On 6 July 1871 he was elected assistant surgeon to St. Thomas's Hospital.

However, in 1876 he resigned the post having determined to concentrate on parish work.

He was ordained deacon in 1878 and was licensed to the curacy at Beckenham where, being ordained priest in 1879, he remained until 1884 when Dr Ellicott, Bishop of Gloucester appointed him vicar of Bussage, Gloucestershire. While here he did much work in the church. His parish clerk, Peter Clissold, said of him: '*The Rev. H. Arnott opened the Church for Worship every day, and it was never locked, so that people could go in at any time to say their prayers. Mr Arnott put a new look on the Church. He got a Chancel Screen and a new Organ and a heating apparatus, as well as a Litany Desk, and a new cover to the font, and a lot of new chairs and kneeling pads'.[50] He also enlarged the Vicarage by adding a large dining-room and kitchen and rooms over them*'.

Arnott was eminently fitted for the pastoral role and throughout his long ministry exercised a widespread influence for good. He was a man of handsome and distinguished presence and his sermons were remarkable for their clear and orderly expression. He held the cure at Bussage until 1885 when he was presented to the living of his old stamping ground in Beckenham by a private patron. Here he remained for thirty-four years until his retirement in 1919.

Henry Arnott died at his house in Rochester on 27 March 1931, aged 88, and was buried at Beckenham; he was survived by four sons and four daughters, his wife, having predeceased him.

---

[50] Lambert

Rev. Irvine Kempt Anderson: 1885-86

Ordained priest in 1884, Rev. Anderson took up the post of Perpetual Curate in Bussage the following year. He is remembered for his introduction of the use of vestments at St Michael's. This was a step away from the Tractarian custom of celebrating in the Anglican tradition of surplice and stole.

Robert Clissold, Parish Clerk for many years, obviously considered this worthy of comment as he is recorded as saying in the Parish Magazine in 1900: 'Mr Anderson came next, and he introduced the coloured Vestments.'

Anderson is shown to be living at Bussage in Crockford's 1887 directory so it appears that he remained in the parish after giving up the living.

Rev. Christopher Smyth: 1886-91

Made deacon in 1850 and priest in 1851, Smyth's first parish was at Woodford, Northants, where 'during a smallpox epidemic he remained with his wife at his post, having sent his young children away, in order that sufferers might receive nursing and attention in the rectory.' He only moved on from there because the income from the glebe land reduced to a level that would not support two clergy and, according to Lambert's history, 'he felt his colleague deserved the living more'. After leaving Woodford, he spent some time in Italy before accepting the post at Bussage in 1886.

It is noted in the October 1896 magazine that the Confraternity of the Blessed Sacrament 'the Ward of St Michael and All Angels, Bussage, was formed in the year 1887 – obviously at the encouragement of Rev. Smyth.

The Confraternity of the Blessed Sacrament (CBS) was founded in 1862 as part of the Catholic Revival in the Church of England. Its aim was to be, first of all, a confraternity (brotherhood) of men and women praying and working for a greater devotion to Jesus Christ in the Eucharist and in the Sacrament of his Body and Blood. This perhaps best demonstrates Smyth's churchmanship.

Rev. Christopher Smyth was a keen Alpine climber and was the first to climb Monte Rosa, the second highest mountain in the Alps and in Western Europe.

He was active at Bussage until 1891 when a fall from a horse made his retirement necessary. 'He continued, however, to live in the neighbourhood, and his house was the centre for every kind of good work for God's glory at home or abroad. He was never so happy as when well enough to help in Bussage Church or at the chapel of the House of Mercy. The influence of his quiet, consistent Christian life is incalculable.[51]' He died at Firwood in December 1900 and was buried in the churchyard at Bussage on Christmas Eve. 'The burial took place at day-break, with solemn requiem; and in spite of the early hour, the little church was filled with a devout congregation, who had come to join in offering the Holy Sacrifice for the repose of the soul of him who had all his life long been a humble servant of God.'[52] His obituary appeared in the Parish Magazine: '... *he was widely known, and*

[51] Obituary in the Parish Magazine

[52] ibid

wherever he was known he was loved. He had been in delicate health for some time, but his unfailing cheerfulness and brightness, even up to the very end, made it difficult to realise that his life on earth was drawing to a close.'

Initially there was an idea to put up a window in the church to his memory but an alternative scheme offered: a contribution towards the Native College in Lebombo where his son was Bishop. Accordingly, the sum of £1,000 was paid to the Native College in Lebombo by the parish as a suitable memorial to Rev. Smyth.

He and his wife, Clementine Royds, had four children – two sons and two daughters. The daughters painted the fresco depicting the Ten Virgins which adorns the Tower.

One son, William Edmund, (1858-1950) became chaplain to the bishop of Zululand following his ordination and subsequently the first bishop of Lebombo (1893 – 1912). He actively maintained the link with Bussage throughout his ministry. The July 1896 edition of the Bussage Parish Magazine notes this connection: 'To Mr Smyth you owe your sympathy with the Lebombo Mission; his interest has enkindled your interest, and his touching words from the pulpit touched the hearts of all who listened.' Bishop Smyth regularly wrote to and visited the people of Bussage.

Rev. William Barker Drawbridge: 1891-95

Made deacon in 1855 and priest in 1856 at York, Drawbridge went to India in 1860 where he worked in Goudad, Berhampore, Nagode & Nowgong, Darjeeling, Dacca, Jubbulpore, Landour, Mutgtra, Cuttack, Barrackpore, Hazareebagh, Cawnpore, Futtegurh.

On his return to the UK, he spent some years in Kent before moving to Bussage. At this time the population of the parish was 382. Rev W.B. Drawbridge celebrated a Solemn Requiem for the Souls of the deceased Founders in 1894.

Robert Suckling's son, then Vicar of St Alban's Holborn, preached at this service.

Rev. Norman Donald Macleod: 1894-05

Deacon (1881) and priest (1882) Rev. N. D. McLeod was a strong Tractarian. He held daily services and encouraged parishioners to adopt a rule of life with frequent reception of Holy Communion encouraged. A strict adherent to the Book of Common Prayer, he had private means that he was happy to use for the support of the parish. He established the Parish Magazine which not only demonstrates his forward thinking but also gives us an invaluable source of information about life in Bussage during this period.

He once claimed that he felt an affinity with the church at Bussage, having served as curate to T C Woollcombe, the son of one of the founders and, it would seem that, for all their faults – and he berates them regularly in the pages of the magazine - he was fond of his congregation. McLeod was, according to Malcolm Lambert, a 'firm, level-headed and kind' man who 'knew the needs of his people'.[53]

It was during his incumbency that the Post Office was introduced to the village (offering savings opportunities), a recreation club was set up for men during the winter, a library was created and the village school went from being poorly attended and low achieving to a well-supported school that garnered excellent reports from the inspectors.

And here perhaps it might be appropriate to mention Mrs E. J. Macleod specifically. Vicars' wives are virtually invisible in the formal records but the work they do in not only supporting their husbands in the privacy of their homes but also in the hands-on work

[53] Lambert ch 6

of the parish (as evidenced by Mrs Smyth in the smallpox epidemic previously mentioned) is immense.

The Parish Magazine enables us to glimpse what Mrs Macleod is actually doing. She instigates a 'Boot Club ... for the benefit of Members, who will receive a bonus of a penny on every shilling', a Coal Club (equally subsidised by her) which entitled members to a ton of coal every winter and a weekly Mothers' group at which fabric was provided for the women to use to sew for their families at a very low cost. She sells Bibles and other religious material at the Vicarage, personally pays for several of the Stations of the Cross and subscribes to other church needs, holds regular Rummage Sales, entertainments, concerts and other activities. She provides a prize for sewing at the school and creates a band consisting of: Pianoforte, Miss Leech; Drum, Mrs Macleod; Rattle, Mrs Sibree; Triangle, Mrs Wheeler; Quail, Miss Smyth; Cuckoo, Miss Z Smyth; Nightingale, Miss Wheeler; Trumpets, Messrs Carroll and Thackwell; Bells, Mr B Carroll; with Miss Rudd as Conductor'. All this despite the fact that she is clearly suffering from a health problem.

In the December 1900 edition of the Magazine, the Rev. Macleod writes: *For some considerable time past, owing to the state of my Wife's health, I have felt it to be my obvious duty either to place my resignation of the Benefice of Bussage in the Bishop's hands, or to seek a longer change and rest than that afforded by a usual Summer holiday.'*
The Bishop was obviously keen for Rev. Macleod to

remain for he sanctioned the Vicar to 'accompany Mrs. Macleod to the Riviera for ten weeks, leaving home on November 27th, and returning in, probably the second week of February'. There is an air of desperation about this – that Rev. Macleod has to threaten to resign in order to be allowed to take his wife away to restore her health suggests a distinct lack of pastoral care amongst the clergy.

However, in 1904 he was offered a living that was too good to refuse and decided that the time had come to leave Bussage. His last message in the magazine appeared in September. He went to all Saints', Narborough-with-Huncote in Leicestershire. There was a presentation to him and his wife on St Michael's day – an illuminated address with the names of all the (72) subscribers appended: an armchair for the Vicar, a pair of silver candlesticks for Mrs Macleod, and a silver-plated tea urn. Rev. Macleod died in Torquay on 18th June 1934.

St Michael and All Angels, Bussage – postcard circa 1890

Rev. Herbert Finzel Hayward: 1905-21

Made deacon in 1891 and priest in 1893, Rev. Hayward was 'a personality' and a gifted organist. He composed a hymn to St Michael that was still being sung in the 1980s at the Patronal Festival and had a quirky sense of humour in that he occasionally played 'It's a long way to Tipperary' as an organ voluntary. There is no record of what the congregation may have thought of this.

At this time the parish was reckoned to contain around 300 souls, most of whom worked in the local mills and Rev. Hayward organised his services around the working hours. In 1908, the Holy Communion service on Ascension Day was at 4.30 a.m. and 30 people took advantage of this.

Very much building on the foundations laid by his predecessor, Hayward was aided by able lay parishioners as he set about beautifying the church. Two women – Miss Cababe and Miss Rudd – a woodcarver and embroiderer respectively, were especially involved in this project.

Miss Cababe (who married the British Vice-Consul to Isfahan in 1910) carved a set of emblems of the saints on shields around the sanctuary in oak and added a sedilia. Miss Rudd not only wrote a history of Bisley - *Historical Records of Bisley with Lypiatt Gloucestershire* (John Jennings, Gloucestershire, 1937) to which this history has several times referred – but was also responsible for making and donating frontals, vestments and also helped make the banner of St Michael for the chancel, encouraged in this work by Rev. Hayward.

In a letter published in the magazine in January 1905, Hayward comments that: 'the name of Bussage has for years been familiar to me in connection with the splendid work done in the cause of teaching and upholding the Catholic Faith.' Hayward was inducted on the 4 February. He is recorded as saying that 'Englishmen seem to expect their Parish Priest to have the saintliness of S. John, the zeal and energy of S. Peter, the statesmanship of S. Paul and the business qualities of a City man!' Clearly he had a pretty good idea of what was expected of him.

Hayward had the misfortune to be in office during the carnage of the First World War in which many men from the local area were actively involved. Wallace Clissold was one of 'the gallant band of 29 serving from Bussage and District'[54]. Aged 20, this 'promising son' – the latest in a long line of Clissold men who served the church in various capacities - was killed in action. The Sunday morning after the news reached his parents, almost every man in the village, together with the local company of the boy

---

[54] https://greatwarchalford.wordpress.com/sifting-the-evidence/page/10/ 15/03/2017 20.56 GMT

scouts, attended the choral Eucharist at the parish church as a mark of esteem.

'The Rev H. F. Hayward, preached a sermon on the text 'a fine soldier' and gave "a loving and touching tribute to the deceased, who from his earliest years had been a member of the choir and a server at the altar right up to the time of his leaving home to join the Guards." He expressed sorrow, but "also consciousness of a duty nobly done."[55]' It cannot have been an easy task consoling the families of the soldiers that did not return.

In 1921, Hayward left Bussage and took a post at St. Mark's, in Kingsholm, Gloucestershire; a church dedicated in the same year as St Michael & All Angels.

Rev. Herbert Pulman Barchard: 1921-44

Ordained Deacon in 1984 and priested in 1895, Barchard was chaplain to the House of Mercy prior to taking the post at St Michael's. His incumbency is commemorated by the Rood carving. It was Barchard who presented the figure of St Michael (see front cover), together with the picture of the Madonna and Child (a copy of Raphael's Sistine Madonna) to St Michael's.

His work centred on Traditional Eucharistic worship with a large choir although he was very serious and not keen on music generally.

---

[55] ibid

 He lived in the Chaplain's House of St Michael's Home as the vicarage (known as Glebe House) was at that time let to a series of tenants purely for the income; by 1944 it was divided into two separate houses and the second let in order to increase the value of the living.

In 1926, men and women were segregated in church and, as a former orphan from St Elizabeth's Home in Eastcombe recalled, the services acquired a formal, church parade 'feel'. Mrs Barchard would gather the Sunday School who took precedence over the orphans who were required to wait outside the church with one of the nuns; even in church there was no respite, with the Kilburn sisters using their brollies to poke any child foolish enough not to concentrate on the service.

The girls from St Michael's Home fared even worse. Not only did they have to walk across the fields to the church but they waited in the porch before being seated in the south aisle where they were very close, perhaps too close, to the choirboys in the vestry. They would sometimes put notes into the cassock pockets of the choir boys!

Like so many of his generation, Rev. Barchard remained in the parish too long (Lambert ch 6). His wife died in 1940 and he soldiered on alone, his 'sermons became diminutive and congregations dropped'. He died in office.

Rev. Richard Birket Abell   1944-57

Deacon in 1910, priest in 1910, Abell worked for many years in London parishes and as a chaplain in the First World War, after which he had a breakdown and was sent to Whiteshill for recuperation. Then he came to Bussage.

Abell would frequently pop in on his parishioners and was treated very much as part of the family.

At the time there were many houses with servants and Abell broke through the 'upstairs/ downstairs' social boundaries, especially in church.

It has been said that he was the best sort of parish priest: practical and hands-on, a Christian who liked people. He revived the life of parish and successfully worked to build the choir up until it comprised 12 boys, 9 men (5 basses, 4 tenors) and 6 women, though the women did not robe but sat by the organ. They sang masses by Maunder, Adlem, Adams, Woodward; and evensong

He was very keen on building up a sense of community and, as a means of achieving this and as a means of filling the sadly depleted coffers of the church, he set up the September fete, allocating jobs to all and sundry as a way of engendering a feeling of inclusion in his flock.

A keen botanist and member of the Botanist Society, Abell collected numerous specimens of rare plants for the Botanist Society. His sister Louisa Abell of Foxcote Manor (the family home) in Gloucestershire, also shared his botanical passion. She was very popular in the parish and close to her brother. The choirboys and other parishioners often went on plant hunting trips with him. On one memorable occasion he took a party on a botany trip to Plinlimon looking for a lobelia; they found it in a marsh but then had trouble pulling the vicar out of the marsh!

A devoted Anglo-Catholic celibate, Rev. Abell died on 4th April 1957 and was buried in the churchyard in Bussage.

Rev. Guy Harrison Stevens: 1957–60

Stevens was made deacon in 1926 and priest in 1927. Initially Curate at All Saints Clapton Park and St Barnabas Pimlico, he was Chaplain at Maadi and Helouan in Egypt 1929-30, chaplain and assistant master at Woodbridge School from 1931-37, then curate of St Peter's, Eaton Square and Vicar of Tong with St John, before coming to Bussage as Perpetual Curate.

Rev. Stevens was often ill, perhaps as a result of his work in Egypt and died on 5th February 1960. He was described to me as 'a very nice person' by Peter Clissold.

Stevens was married to Dorothea (Dae) Irene Howells Stevens. She outlived him by twenty years and they are both buried in the churchyard at Bussage.

Rev. Hubert George Goddard: 1960-65

Deacon - 1940, priest - 1941, Goddard spent most of his ministry in UK parishes before becoming Perpetual Curate at Bussage. The Crockfords' directory shows him living in Bournemouth in 1969. Rev H.G. Goddard appears to have been shy and lonely, and is reputed to have had great difficulty in managing the parish. A bachelor, he lived with his mother for years before moving to Bussage.

Rev. Alfred Tom Gainey : 1965-68

Deacon 1962 and priest 1963, Gainey was Curate at Bisley for three years before becoming Curate in Charge at Bussage from whence he went on to become vicar at Saul with Fretherne and Framilode. During his incumbency the cure of St Augustine in Eastcombe was added to the parish (1965).

Gainey is reported as being a pleasant, friendly man. He was originally a gardener on the Misenden estate, became a reader at the local church, and sought ordination. He was married to the local district nurse, Wynn, and they had two daughters – one went into the navy and the other married.

Although Gainey was not considered to be a great preacher, he was an excellent parish priest – very much a man of the people. He joined the skittles team at the pub, for example, and was very 'hands on'; known in the parish as Tom.

When he moved in, the men doing his removals were hot and needed a drink so Tom, smoking his pipe, took himself off to the Ram, introduced himself and asked for several crates of beer. He definitely had the common touch and remembered names of all those he met. However, the middle class families, known as 'Ladybodies' didn't approve of him because he wasn't an Oxbridge man! This is probably why he didn't get to stay in Bussage.

Rev. James Arthur Johnson: 1968-75

Deacon 1933, priest, 1934, Johnson was Curate at St Stephen's, Upton Park before joining the UMCA Mission in Msumba in 1936.

He became priest in charge at Kota-Kota and Songea where he worked until 1942 when he returned to the UK.

Johnson was married and had a daughter, Janet. He was considered rather aloof, not the sort of person you would go to with a problem and was not overly interested in the choir.

According to Malcolm Lambert, Johnson diminished the 'despotism' of Janet Johnson who with Dorothea Marion Beale (related to the Beale of Cheltenham College) ran Bussage House as a school for clergy daughters. Despite this, Miss Johnson appears to have been incorrigible in her determination to do what she could for the homeless in the area taking them into Bussage House so that the local authority would have to do something about their plight. School newsletters show that her pupils had a genuine respect for her despite or perhaps because of her legendary formidable character.

Rev. Stephen Robert (John) Stevens: 1975-84

Born in 1914, Stevens was made deacon in 1966 and priest in 1967. By the time he became Vicar of Bussage he was heading for retirement. He was married and had an adult son.

Known to all and sundry as 'John', prior to ordination he worked for the Ministry of Agriculture and Fisheries as an inspector.

Bussage was his only parish and it seems that even if he was lacking in experience he was certainly not lacking in enthusiasm.

Rev S. R. Stevens restored St Augustine's, installing a permanent concrete floor (replacing chipboard), laying carpet and replacing the old pews with light wooden chairs. Gas heating was added and two stained-glass figures inserted into the east window. These depicted St Augustine and St Aidan, representing the Roman and Celtic missionary traditions that Christianised Britain in the 7th Century. Stevens also oversaw the building of a new School in Bussage on land purchased by the Diocese when the new housing estate was first mooted.

Stevens appears to have been a cheerful and untiring man, loving children and instigating children's services, he also cared for the poor, sick and old of his parish.

St Augustine of Canterbury, Eastcombe

During his time, the Manor Farm estate was developed, considerably increasing both the size of the parish and the workload of the priest.

Rev. Herbert John van der Linde: 1984-13

Originally from South Africa and one of twins, van der Linde was made deacon in 1968, and priest in 1969; he spent half his working life as Vicar of Bussage, retiring in 2013.

During his incumbency, he instigated the move which meant that Bussage became a Forward in Faith Parish. This effectively isolated the parish, cutting it off from both the Benefice of Bisley and the Diocese of Gloucester. Van de Linde actively objected to the ordination of women and was a signatory to a letter addressed to the Archbishops of Canterbury and York in 2008.[56]

His wife, Felicity, has been described as a nice lady, musically gifted, who was good with people.

They have a son who has followed his father into the ministry.

St Michael and All Angels' church became one of the ninety-six parishes nationwide which were overseen by the Bishop of Ebbsfleet, a "flying bishop" appointed in 1994 to provide episcopal oversight for parishes which had issues with accepting the ordination of women.

The current edition of Crockford's reports Rev. van der Linde to be living in Cricklade and the internet reports that he is an assistant priest at St Mark's Church in Swindon.

Despite Rev. van der Linde's obvious sincerity and commitment, it was left to his successor to pick up and carry forward the work of pastoral outreach that

[56] See Appendix III

had been started by Rev. Stevens with the new community who had moved into the new Manor Farm estate.

Following the departure of van de Linde, the Bussage and Eastcombe Churches were reintegrated into the Gloucester Diocese and the parish was able to take its place in the Bisley Benefice which had been formed in 2004. The first Benefice Vicar was Rev. Rosie Woodall followed in 2018 by Rev. Susan Murray.

Rev. Michael David Clark: 2015-18

Created deacon in 1972 and priest in 1973, Rev. Mike Clark achieved an MA in Geography at Oxford University prior to taking holy orders.

Subsequent to a curacy in Cheadle, Cheshire he went as a missionary to Brazil (1977-86), following which he went to work in Bolivia (86-88).

Mike was Commissary to the Diocese of Angola for five years and, ironically enough considering the links between St Michael's and Lebombo, he worked with Bishop Dinis Sengulane (Bishop of Lebombo 1976 - 2014) in the setting up the new Diocese of Angola. As commissary, Mike was a sort of ambassador, representing the first Bishop of Angola, Rt Revd Andre Soares and looking after his interests. In his own words: 'When I first felt God's call to work with Angola, all the agencies like USPG knew about it was that there was a 42-year old war going on. It was all in Portuguese and there were rumours of a people-movement in the North among the Bakongos started in the early 1920s.' Needless to say, there was a lot more to the situation than this which led to some extremely hair-raising and dangerous expeditions for the unknown, ecclesiastical 'Indiana Jones' that ended up in Bussage!

Surviving his African adventures, Clark later worked in Wilton, Tollington, London, and Edgware (where he converted the grapes growing in his neighbour's garden into vast quantities of wine – another passion of his) before taking the role of curate in the Benefice of Bisley, which now comprised Bisley, Chalford, France Lynch, Oakridge and Bussage with Eastcombe.

A committed evangelist, Clark worked hard to build up the congregation of St Michael's and encouraged outreach in the parish, frequently using lay involvement. In 2017 he oversaw a highly successful Alpha Course and the subsequent setting up of home study groups in Eastcombe and Bussage.

His wife, Lois, daughter of US missionaries and brought up in South America, worked tirelessly beside her husband to spread the Gospel. A gentle, generous, unassuming woman with a quirky sense of humour, Lois threw herself into the life of the parish, regularly attending home groups and becoming a valued member of the Open the Book team that dramatised Bible stories at the primary school assemblies, as well as undertaking numerous unsung acts of kindness. She loved to share her skill at making beautiful ice candles. On many occasions, she would use tales of her life as a child of a missionary in Peru to add colour and depth to discussions of faith, showing a range of experience very far removed from the microcosm of British life that is Bussage.

By the time Mike and Lois arrived in Bussage, their four children were grown up, though two of them presented their proud parents with grandchildren during their time in Gloucestershire. Mike Clark left the village upon his extremely well-earned retirement.

Chapter 7 - The House of Mercy

House of Mercy staff and friends

The House of Mercy was founded in 1851 by the Rev. Robert Suckling, first Vicar of Bussage, together with Bishop Armstrong of Grahamstown, and Mrs. Grace Anne Poole, at the latter's expense, to house 26 girls, aged 14-18 years, whose lamentable home backgrounds necessitated moral and domestic training. Ostensibly set up to house 'fallen women', the inmates included those considered to be sexually promiscuous, working in prostitution or, as was frequently the case, unmarried mothers, a condition that was totally beyond the pale socially at the time. The House of Mercy aimed to provide education alongside spiritual, moral and domestic training. Grace Poole was specifically requested to undertake this work by Rev Robert Suckling and Bishop Armstrong.

Armstrong was unquestionably the originator of the

Church Penitentiary movement and, in his lengthy correspondence with Mr Ford, he makes it clear that he considers society, and specifically the Church, to have neglected its duty towards these 'erring daughters'. He recognised the need to do more than just train 'fallen' women for work, being concerned for their spiritual wellbeing. "I am strongly in favour of an auxiliary Hospice in some colony under clerical control, where we might draft off the promising Penitents, and secure them a fresh start in good places and families, instead of exposing them to the worse places at home, where bad pay and hard work might again break down their virtue." But he recognised the scale of the challenge and determined to start small, considering that "to commence with a house full of such women would break the heart and spirit of any man".

In August 1850, Armstrong became acquainted with Robert Suckling of Bussage. Their friendship was deep and intense although they were singularly unalike. It was during a short visit they made to the late Bishop of Gloucester and Bristol that they had a "midnight talk," when the idea of the House of Mercy at Bussage was fully discussed, and Rev. Suckling offered to undertake its spiritual superintendence.

The work was commenced in a small cottage belonging to Mr. Suckling, in April, 1851. On the sixth of October of that same year, Mr. Armstrong was present at the anniversary festival of the consecration of the church at Bussage. It was to be their last meeting as not long afterwards Suckling died. But, Armstrong fought on with the idea. He aimed to employ self-sufficient, devoted Christian women instead of paid matrons, which is where Grace Anne Poole and the creation of a Sisterhood come into the picture. He felt that it was manifestly impossible for 'ladies' to bear the burden of such works without the sympathy and support of other like-minded women. He also recognised that a constituted authority and fixed rule would enable order and continuity, thus, a form of Anglican Sisterhood arose.

A firm believer in the Oxford Movement and the social care that was embedded in that creed, Mrs Poole saw this work as an opportunity to demonstrate her belief that one should do good, not only in the parish, but also in the wider world. One cannot help but think that it must have been a shock to her when she saw the conditions in Bussage. However, her faith was central to her character and she was fearless in doing what she considered God required of her.

The young women living in the House of Mercy were expected to be regular in their attendance at church and, as a consequence, it soon became apparent there was not sufficient space at St Michael and All Angels to accommodate them. Thus, the south aisle, designed by George Frederick Bodley RA, an English Gothic Revival architect, was added. But that was not all. As Peter Drover states in his work for the Chalford Parish Local History Group: 'A fully attended meeting of the Churchwardens and Sidesmen held in 1895 and chaired by the Vicar unanimously adopted the resolution *'That until*

*notice is given to the contrary, on Sunday evenings
the seats shall be allotted thus – South and side
aisles for men and boys, North aisle and West end for
women and girls''*

Around 1859, her close friend, Canon Keble (son of
the Thomas Keble who founded St Michael's
church), took her to Hursley to visit his uncle the
Rev. John Keble, a prime mover and shaker in the
Tractarian movement, and she spent two days there,
afterwards saying that the help and encouragement
she received from him at this time was one of her
most treasured memories – a source of support that
continued. She shared a close friendship with the
Canon's wife, Mrs Keble, was Godmother to their
son who became Rev. George Keble, and regarded
their daughter, who helped her in her penitentiary
work, almost as a daughter.

When taking into account the inferior status of
women generally in society at this time, it is perhaps
notable that Grace Anne counted amongst her friends
the founder of Bussage church, the Rev. Thomas
Keble and his son, Rev. Isaac Williams, another
pillar of the Tractarian movement, the then Bishop of
Gloucester, who 'she regarded as a true friend',
sundry other notable members of the church
hierarchy and clergy like Rev. Henry Arnott, Rev.
Christopher Smyth and Rev. I K Anderson all of
whom had occupied the incumbency of Bussage
themselves. But her friends were not limited to the
various professional and prosperous people she
encountered through her work, local village families
were just as important to her; Rev. Suckling

mentions her friendship circle embracing many of members of local Bussage families such as Gardiner, Bird, Eddels, Trotman, Pincott, Bingle, Price, Kirby, Marmont and 'Thomas Cox the book hawker'.

Rev. Suckling (Junior) comments in his eulogy printed in the Parish Magazine at her death, that she not only ran the House of Mercy, but will also be remembered for 'her care of the sick, her walks to Stroud to visit the Poor in the Workhouse …her large class in the Sunday School', her hard work for the Choir, not only as organist but also for the printing of the hymns used in the church which were 'set up and typed off by herself'. 'Her liberality to the sick and aged was felt to be one of those many tokens of her friendship and of a life lived for other people'.

The list of attendees at her funeral reads almost as a Who's Who of Tractarian influence. The names recorded include members of the Hopton family, representatives of the Suckling and Keble families, several previous incumbents of Bussage Church, together with women from the Community she had served for so long and pall bearers taken from the village families. At her funeral, Rev. Suckling reports that 'one of the bearers wished to undertake that last act of respect for her, because her nursing had saved his life when a child'

The House of Mercy was begun in Kirby's Cottage, near the grounds of Brownshill House. Originally, there were 25 inmates with staff and Sisters, a chapel dedicated to St Michael and All Angels and a laundry. 'This work was, by its very nature, one that could not be spoken much about. The existence of such a work at that time was in itself a wonder in the neighbourhood, and a subject of mystery, because there were such a variety of accounts as to what was being done, and so little true information was able to be made public. The exaggerations were most perplexing; they would hardly be believed if now stated.'[57]

The early death of Rev. Robert Suckling in November 1851 seems to have had a positive impact on the work, possibly bringing it to public attention by association, but whatever the cause, there was a definite increase in the respect and admiration for the work amongst the general public. The death of Bishop Armstrong not long after must have been a massive blow for Grace Anne, but she did not allow this to impact on the work.

'This work was, by its very nature, one that could not be spoken much about. The existence of such a work at that time was in itself a wonder in the neighbourhood, and a subject of mystery, because there were such a variety of accounts as to what was being done, and so little true information was able to be made public. The exaggerations were most perplexing; they would hardly be believed if now stated.'[58]

---

[57] Rev. Suckling Junior, Parish Mag. July 1896

[58] Rev. Suckling, Parish Mag. July 1896

Plaque dedicated to Grace Anne Poole in St Michael and All
Angel's Church

It says much that upon the death of Mrs. Poole in
1900 the work of the House faltered and, shortly
after, the Wantage Community of Sisters undertook
management. In the 1920s Sr Sylvia Mary, one of
the Wantage sisters, described it as: 'a training home
for girls who needed protection; a few were
delinquents and rather simple-minded' going on to
describe happy expeditions into the Cotswolds.
However, in 1947 they withdrew their Superior and
Laundry Sister and, in 1949, the Home was forced to
close down. It was given to the Society of the
Incarnation of Birmingham for charitable work of the
Church of England and in 1959, the site was sold to
the Servants of the Paraclete, who had operated a
spiritual healing ministry in Brownshill since 1923,
and the work of the trustees was completed when the
proceeds of the trust were paid into the Church Moral
Aid Association.

Caroline Hopton, a Sister of Mercy.
Photographed by T. Jones of Hereford and Ludlow.

This portrait of Caroline Annie Hopton, who was a Sister of Mercy working with Grace Anne Poole, her aunt, shows the uniform worn by the Sisters. Born at Montreal in Canada in or about 1850, Caroline was the daughter of Charles Edward Hopton, (Grace Anne's brother) who was a Captain in the 23rd Welsh Fusiliers, and his wife Mary Jane née Vaughan. Caroline Hopton died at Brownshill House on 9 January 1934, aged 84. She left effects valued at £2597. According to the abstract of her will, probate was granted to her brother Charles Ernest Hopton, Archdeacon of Birmingham.

Grace Anne Poole

Born on the 14 March 1808 in Whitchurch, Bucks, Grace Anne was the eldest child of Rev. John Hopton of Canon Frome in Herefordshire. She was named Grace Anne after her mother, who reputedly suffered from a delicate constitution although this did not prevent her from giving birth to several children. In October 1839, the Rev. J. Hopton's wife, Grace Anne's mother, died aged 53 at Canon Frome Court. Her father died in December 1870 aged 88.

From a very early age, Grace Anne was required to 'be a little mother' to the other children and, according to Rev. Suckling Junior, she recalled being told: 'a great girl like you should be of use' when she was a mere two years of age. This comment obviously had a great influence on Grace and it was during her childhood that she acquired 'the strength of will, power of ruling, courage, reverence for authority, gratitude for kindnesses, brightness, sympathy with and interest in others, together with the faculty of making friends' that her later work would require.

Always an early riser, she considered lying in bed to be wasted time, she was renowned for her cheerfulness and courage. Even in her last days, she amazed her visitors by her uncomplaining gratitude for all being done for her.

According to Suckling, she was a little over thirty when she left home in September 1841 to marry James Poole of the Homend, Ledbury. However, despite the geographical distance now separating them, she kept very close links with her brothers and sisters and one of her nieces became a Sister at the House. 'Brownshill House was the residence of Mrs Poole during her married life, but when she became a widow she resided at the House of Mercy as Mother Superior, till her death, and Brownshill house became the home of the various chaplains of the Community.'[59]

---

[59] Rudd p 354

Chapter 8 – Village Life 1895-1905

The Parish Magazine

The first edition of the Parish Magazine appeared in October 1895 at a cost of 1d per edition although the outlay of 4½d (slightly less than 5p) would get you three editions, post free. Rev. Macleod, the inspiration behind it, explained what he hoped to achieve with the project:

To start a Magazine in a small Parish like ours is a venturesome thing to do. Local events of interest or of importance are fewer than in a larger place, and parish news cannot be made out of nothing. (Parish gossip can; but this is a very different matter, and we hope it will never find an entrance into these pages.) ... this will probably be done at a loss – the cost will probably exceed the receipts. But if all our parishioners and friends subscribe, and if some are kind enough to take extra copies to distribute elsewhere, the loss will not be serious and will be worth meeting.

He was certainly accurate in his assumption that the magazine would run at a loss and the subsequent issues are littered with regular reminders that subscriptions were due, that more subscribers needed to be found or that contributions to reduce the deficit were required.

The Bussage Magazine, as it was initially called, was

intended to consist of two parts. As Macleod goes on to explain: 'one of these, called "The Dawn of the Day" is published in London by the S.P.C.K.[60] ...we believe they will be found helpful and interesting. The other is the parochial part, which will give full information about the Services of the Church and things connected therewith.'[61]   It is this latter part that has been retained. It was also said that the Magazine would give the Vicar 'opportunities to tell us about various matters which may not always be suited to the pulpit' as well as chronicling local events. It is not clear who the editors are, though one imagines that Rev. Macleod was one of them.

Macleod left the parish in October 1904 and in the November edition it was announced that the Rev. F. D Robinson would take charge of the parish during the interregnum, staying at Brownshill House. However, by December the Rev. Herbert Finzel Hayward had been appointed. The Rev. Robinson went to Christ Church, Clapton, a parish in the East End of London.   Hayward continued with the magazine but it is noticeable that the tone of the publication changed dramatically becoming more chatty though no less rigorous in its practical Christianity. From the evidence in the copies that remain, it is possible to peep into the personalities and lives of the these men.

From a historian's point of view, having access to the Parish Magazines is a priceless gift as copies of a

---

[60] Society for Promoting Christian Knowledge

[61] October 1895 Parish Magazine

relatively ephemeral publication such as those is invaluable in providing a snapshot of the everyday facts of life in a small village over a period of ten years as they chronicle the changes that the people of the area experienced during that time. In an effort to collate these entries to tell a coherent story of what it was like to live in Bussage during these years, and adding in facts which explain the context of these against a wider picture, I have gathered together the data under various headings: education, recreation, welfare, missionary work, behaviour issues, church, social change and a catch-all – humour and oddities. There is much I have left out but I hope you find the following as fascinating as I have.

One aspect of village life that the magazines shed a powerful light on is the involvement of the Vicar's wife. These usually unnamed, virtually invisible women not only supplied everyday support for their husbands so that the work of the church could move forward – and at times that must have been uphill work! - but they frequently took on a vital role requiring all the skills of a social worker, the practical, hands-on support for families in the form of clothing and fuel, and a full-time, parish fund-raiser. She would also be expected to be a paragon and example to the women of the village in her role as a mother and housekeeper, as well as providing endless refreshments for the various activities taking place in her home. The work the clergy wives did was immeasurably important and yet these women are rarely recognised for the proficient managers they clearly were. To my mind, the fact that they were content to serve in this way is as valid an example of

Christian values being put into action as that provided by their far more visible husbands. I find it truly sad that we don't even know the names of so many of them.

Within the pages of the magazines I found hints of the everyday stories of people who lived in the village ranging from their reaction to great events like the death of Queen Victoria to the incredibly touching and stark notices relating to baptisms and deaths like these:

Vivian Charles Elphinston Robertson was baptised on St Stephen's Day, 26th December 1896. His father, John, Elphinston Robertson (24 yrs), died suddenly on that day. The family were from Richmond.

Charles Mark Coggins was baptised on 30 April 1904 (privately). He was the son of William and Gertrude Coggins and, sadly, died on the 1st May aged 3 weeks.

July 1901 and another reminder of the infant mortality that was so much a part of life at this time: C(K)atherine Elsie Pincott – baptised May 9th, died June 11th aged 4 months.

Items of ordinary everyday life also appear:

'A dark fur boa has for some time been lying unclaimed in Church. Should this meet the eye of the owner, she may be glad to know that her property can be obtained on applying to the Parish Clerk.'

(April 1900)

One can only surmise as to the fate of the boa!

Education

In 1895, the village school was a National School. This meant that it had been set up under the scheme devised by the National Society for Promoting Religious Education which was founded on 16 October 1811 on the premise that "the National Religion should be made the foundation of National Education, and should be the first and chief thing taught to the poor, according to the excellent Liturgy and Catechism provided by our Church." Realistically, this meant that the schools were implemented by the local vicar and members of the Church of England who would frequently provide what financial support they could.

In 1833 Parliament authorised the provision of money for the construction of schools for poor children of England and Wales and a succession of Acts followed which helped to expand the scope of education a little, but most education was still in the hands of churches and philanthropists, and there was really no unified education system. It should be noted that it was considered more important for boys to be educated than for girls, who were often taught sewing while the boys were taught more academic subjects. In fact, there was a specific grant to fund needlework for the girls and prizes presented annually for the best pupils.

Teaching was mainly by rote with emphasis particularly placed on learning to read and write. In some areas there was a constant battle between the aims of the school to teach and the needs of parents who relied on the help of their children so many pupils did not turn up for lessons. Parents were often required to contribute in order for their children to attend school, or at least to supply paper, ink and other requirements, and this could be a real barrier in poor families. Sadly, this is still the case in some parts of the world today where the same difficulties exist.

However, by 1880 additional legislation meant that, by law, UK children had to attend school between the ages of 5 and 10 although some local discretion was allowed including adjusting school hours in agricultural areas. Parents of children who did not attend school could be fined. There were exemptions for illness, living more than a certain distance (typically one mile) from a school, or certification providing proof that the child had reached the required standard.

The Standards of Education from 1872

Six Standards of Education were set out in the Revised code of Regulations, 1872. These standards do not correspond to year groups, in Victorian times promotion was on merit, and many children did not complete all the grades. This is what the children were required to do:

STANDARD I

Reading: Read one of the narratives in an elementary reading book used in the school.

Writing: Copy in manuscript handwriting a line of print, and write from dictation a few common words.

Arithmetic: Simple addition and subtraction of numbers of not more than four figures, and the multiplication table to multiplication by six.

STANDARD II

Reading: Read a short paragraph from an elementary reading book.

Writing: Write a sentence from the same book, slowly read once, and then dictated in single words.

Arithmetic: The multiplication table, and any simple rule as far as short division.

STANDARD III

Reading: Read a short paragraph from a more advanced reading book.

Writing: Write a sentence slowly dictated once by a few words at a time, from the same book.

Arithmetic: Long division, compound rules, money.

STANDARD IV

Reading: Read a few lines of poetry or prose, at the choice of the inspector.

Writing: Write a sentence slowly dictated once, by a few words at a time, from a reading book such as is used in the first class of the school.

Arithmetic: Compound rules (common weights and measures).

STANDARD V

Reading: Read a short ordinary paragraph in a newspaper, or other modern narrative.
Writing: Another short ordinary paragraph in a newspaper, or other modern narrative, slowly dictated once by a few words at a time.
Arithmetic: Practice and bills of parcels.

STANDARD VI

Reading: Read with fluency and expression.
Writing: Write a short theme or letter, or an easy paraphrase.
Arithmetic: Proportion and fractions (vulgar and decimal).

It was one of Thomas Keble's primary aims that a school should be set up for Bussage children and a building was provided near the church for this purpose. Such schools were inspected on a regular basis by both the Diocese and the Government.

In 1895 the first edition of the Parish Magazine reports that the school in Bussage was not meeting the required criteria. However, by October of that year, the School 'had passed through a severe crisis … Her Majesty's Inspector visited the School on October 11ᵗʰ … the award given is 'Good'.' The terrors of OFSTED are nothing new! It appears that the improvements were due to the appointment of a new head teacher and this is reflected in the December edition where the following report appears:

Mr Harrison has, during the short time that he has

been in charge, greatly improved this School. The attainments of the older children are more or less good throughout, and the history as well as the arithmetic of the Fifth Standard deserves great praise. A higher level of attainments should be aimed at with the Infants, though what they profess to do they do well.'

The Grant on the Total Average Attendance amounts to 18/- for each child, exclusive of the Grant for Needlework.

With reference to the Attendance Grant, it cannot be too strongly impressed upon Parents that its total amount depends to a very great extent upon them. ... the sum allotted depends upon the average number of children present on each occasion that the School is opened. In our School, for instance, although there are about 60 children on the books, these Grants have been paid for 46 children only, for only that number attended School on an average during the past year. Fourteen children have therefore been educated for nothing; had these fourteen been present on each occasion, then the school would have gained 14 times 18s more than it did ... Parents should never keep their children from school without some good reason, and should always bear in mind that the better their children attend, the better for all concerned.

What this report highlights is that the funding for the school was dependent very much on the regular attendance of the children and reminders on this theme recur regularly in the Magazine. For many years, there were prizes for children who attended regularly which just goes to highlight the scale of the problem. In December 1895, the following children were presented with prizes for punctual and regular attendance.

Standard V – Arthur Davis

Standard III – Ernest Fawkes, Beatrice Bingle

Standard II – Lizzie Davis, Maud Bingle, Lizzie Bingle

Standard I – Cleave Clissold, Gardiner Clissold, Arthur Beard, Kate Beard

Infants – Ernest Stafford, Grace Clissold, Helen Harrison, Henry Bingle

The same surnames reappear time after time in reports of this kind.

With the school economy in such a precarious state, regular fund-raising events were held to provide necessary funds. The school was also used for social events, being the only building in the village (apart from the Church) which was large enough for such a purpose. An overview of some of these, presents an interesting insight into the entertainments and events that villagers could expect to enjoy. For example, December 1895 saw 'The Great Oriental Fair 'so ably organized and so successfully carried out' which raised £78 for the school.

February 1896 and a letter is printed in the Magazine from head of school appealing to parents to ensure their children attend regularly, punctually and in good appearance.

1896 was obviously an important year for the head

teacher of the school as is shown by notice of the Baptism on Sunday 2ᵘᵈ Feb 1896 of Phyllis Kathleen – daughter to Edward George and Mary Elizabeth Harrison. His wife would doubtless have taken the second class at the school. It was common practice to employ a married couple with the wife teaching the infants.

One can imagine the pleasure (and proud relief) felt when the following appeared in the April 1896 Magazine: 'the Diocesan Inspector has written to say that … he is unable to visit … this year. … this is a sign that the Inspector feels confidence in the Religious Instruction given in our National School.'

But the situation changes and, when the school opens on 31 August, there is a new Master and Mistress in charge – Mr and Mrs Stace. 'Mr Harrison having, with the Vicar's sanction, applied for and obtained the Mastership of the National School at Corby … a village near his own home.' 'We part with Mr and Mrs Harrison with sincere regret, it is difficult to over-estimate the value of the services rendered to the School …' 'The Vicar hopes that all the Day School children will be present when the School opens'. The September edition for 1896 reports that the school rooms have been repainted during the holidays and an appeal for donations for new pictures to be hung on the walls is made.

Obviously the new Master and Mistress have a positive effect as it is reported in December 1896 that the HM Inspector made a very favourable report and 'the higher grant is again awarded and the school is exempted from Inspection until October 1898'. In practical terms, this means that the funding of the school is guaranteed at the same rate ... as long as any impromptu inspection finds that everything is as it should be – which makes keeping the attendance figures steady even more important. A bitter reminder that the school lost £10 in the last year due to bad attendance ends the otherwise positive report in the Magazine.

The Standard in Drawing has lately been so high that comparatively few Schools are classed as "Excellent" and the highest praise is therefore due to both Teachers and Scholars for obtaining this distinction for the Bussage National School.

But in March of 1897 the Magazine records that Mr and Mrs Stace have announced their resignation. 'An offer, unexpected and unsought, has been made to them, which for many reasons it appears advisable to accept.' A Mr and Mrs Phillips are appointed to replace them but their tenure is short-lived and, in July, it is announced that 'Mr William Eden has been appointed Head Master of the National School, with Miss Eden as Assistant. Both are strongly recommended and we hope that in their new teachers the children will find good friends.' A further report in August states that 'Under Mr Eden's care, the School seems to be rapidly regaining the position it had attained under Mr Stace.' One cannot help but think that that Mr and Mrs Phillips were extremely unsatisfactory. No mention is made of why they left so precipitately – taking up the role in April and being gone by July - and one can only speculate.

The October edition reports on a surprise visit by the HM Inspector – who finds 'everything in good order … the attendance seems to have recovered'.

However, the disruption caused by the changes has not escaped the attention of the Inspector and in December the following appears in the Magazine: The Report of the inspector not only deplores the 'injurious effect of frequent change of Teachers' but also says improvement is required in attendance of infants. On top of that, new desks are needed. These were provided in May 1898.

The school is in debt to the sum of £46 16s (£4,000 in today's money) which the Vicar has paid to avoid the cost being laid on the Parish. None of the parents contribute towards the cost of educating their children and it is suggested that a payment of 1s or 2s 6d per quarter be levied on each household. If the school were to close, Chalford civil parish would be liable for the education of the children of Bussage.

Mr Eden's resignation is announced in March 1898. Mr David Heaton, Assistant Master of the Melksham National School, is quickly appointed but as he is not yet married, Miss Florence Wood will assist until Easter when his marriage will take place.

A letter is printed in the Magazine in October 1898 from Rev. Fred. J. Price which demonstrates the far reaching effect of the village school. He writes: 'I am much interested in Bussage because I went to School there, and I may say I got my first glimpses of Catholic Truth in connection with the little Church there, of which I have a photograph before me as I write.' He was writing from St Alban's Rectory, N. Perth, Australia.

However, the School funds are seriously in the red: £33 12s (£3,000) which has (again) been made up by the vicar in order 'to provide for the necessary education of the children.' Mrs Macleod is reported to be getting up 'a series of Entertainments each month during the Winter' and the profits from these will go to the school.

This note is accompanied by yet another reminder that absent children mean less money for the school and a meeting is being called 'with the view of placing the matter more plainly before people and obtaining the sympathy and help of those in whose interests the school is maintained.' Sadly, this meeting was poorly attended and although the following month (December 1898) the Magazine reported that 'the School has gained the highest possible Grant and is again exempt from examination', the parishioners are reminded that 'the Government Grant is paid on the average attendance, so that every time a child is absent from School a certain amount of money is lost. Had all the Scholars attended as regularly as those whose names we published last month, the Grant would have been about £10 more. A real wrong is done to the School when children are kept away on some frivolous pretext.'

1899 sees the school's financial position little improved despite efforts like that of the entertainment where 'Mr Frank Law, who, dressed as a nigger (sic) minstrel, delighted us with his 'Coon' songs' and provided £2 10s (£180) for school funds.

There is a plea in March for subscribers to support the school and 'prevent a School Board, with its secular education and costliness, from being thrust upon us'. By February 1900 the situation is becoming desperate. 'Unfortunately the small size of our School compels us to look elsewhere than to Government ... for [financial] support. Could we provide 80 scholars the case would be different but with an average attendance of under 50 we are compelled to rely on Voluntary Subscriptions for our principal source of income.' Chalford has become a School Board District so maintaining the independence of Bussage School is going to become more difficult. A School Rate is levied on every household in the area.

But they soldier on and by April 1900 'some useful additions have lately been made to the furniture of the National School. The dilapidated Teacher's Desk, which had been in use as long as any one can remember, has been replaced by one more suited to modern requirements, and new Blackboards and Easel have also been provided.' However ever more money is required: 'the Bell Turret at the School ... the wood of which it was built having rotted to such an extent that the whole erection was in danger of collapsing.' Grants from Diocesan Association and the Bishop's church and school fund 'have enabled us to rebuild the Turret as strongly as ever.'

January 1901 and there is a new Curriculum to be instigated at the school. 'Briefly summed up, the New Code might very suitably be prefaced with the words "Intelligence and Character" … until recently the children … were prepared for Examination … now, this preparation for examination is not essential. The New Code … contains much that is interesting; it is full of encouragement … the cultivation of the Reasoning facility is the essential part of education … a complete revolution of our educational system.'

Perhaps more importantly, 'a child is now forbidden by law to work during school hours, whether in the street or workshop, unless exempt from school attendance, and to be exempt a child must either have attended until of full age i.e. 14 years of age; or must have reached a certain Standard of Proficiency' passing the Labour Certificate Examination. This perhaps explains why attendance by some children over the years was so erratic; the children were working.

By the end of the year, subscriptions have been sufficient to keep the school going. Attendance is increasing and the report of inspectors is expected to be good.

1903 and everything changes again. The Education Act, also known as the Balfour Act, was a highly controversial Act of Parliament that set the pattern of elementary education in England and Wales for four decades. The Act provided funds for denominational religious instruction in voluntary elementary schools and ended the divide between voluntary schools, which were largely administered by the Church of England, and schools provided and run by elected school boards. Generally speaking the church schools were (as in Bussage) poorly funded and did not receive money from local tax despite the fact they educated a third of the school children. At the same time local borough or county councils were invested as local education authorities (LEAs) which could set local tax rates. The LEAs could establish new secondary and technical schools as well as developing the existing system of elementary schools. They were in charge of paying teachers, ensuring the teachers were properly qualified and responsible for providing necessary books and equipment. They paid the teachers working in the church schools, with the churches continuing to maintain school buildings and provide religious instruction.

In Bussage, this means that a new board of management will be appointed in March and by June the school has a new name: Bussage Voluntary School. However, it is still relying on contributions to maintain the building and by December is entirely dependent on subscriptions.

On a more prosaic note, mumps closes the school for three weeks which results in the cancellation of the Children's Flower Show. In December 1903 the County Education Committee decrees that attendance prizes should be discontinued. One would like to think that this is because they are no longer required, but the problem of regular attendance at school continues to haunt us today so this is, I feel, unlikely.

May 1904 and the school is closed because of whooping cough. This is the third epidemic of illness to close the school and a stark reminder of the daily battles parents had with diseases we no longer consider dangerous because of the benefits of immunisation. There is no record of what damage these diseases, measles, mumps and whooping cough may have had on the children in Bussage; how many suffered life-changing consequences or even died. However, a note in the April 1896 Magazine highlights this problem. 'It is an open secret that Gloucester has for some time past been suffering from an epidemic of small-pox of considerable severity … For some 10 years past vaccination has been practically neglected in Gloucestershire … thus a large population of several thousands of unvaccinated children exists … as to the mortality, from the 1st January up to March 9th (10 weeks only) 38 deaths have occurred from small-pox … Of these 38 deaths 26 are the deaths of children under ten, all unvaccinated. … Prevention is in the hands of everyone. … there is a grave and urgent and fatal danger to persons or children not vaccinated at all. Nothing changes!

November 1904 – A massive game-changer for the children of the village is announced: eight boys 'of an age and capable of receiving manual instruction' applied to the Education Committee for permission to attend a carpentry class in Brimscombe Polytechnic. The February 1905 edition reports that this was (eventually) agreed and the boys now attend these classes.

January 1905 and Mr Heaton resigns from the school – he and his wife are going to King Stanley School. A presentation is made of a very handsome marble clock and a beautiful silver-plated teapot However, it is not easy finding a suitable replacement and so temporary teachers are put in place: Mrs Morris (ex head of Rylands College) and Miss Butler. Fortunately, by March, George Yardley has been appointed as head. His wife will, naturally, teach the infants.

Recreation

The organisation of entertainments and Treats (as they were called) is another side-effect of the undertakings of the incumbent and his wife who are so very active behind the scenes. Remember, this is the so-called 'Golden Age' when people made their own entertainment and the simple Treats would have been a matter of excitement in such a world. To modern ears they sound simplistic and even bucolic but they must be put into the context of the unrelenting tedium of everyday life as enjoyed by the majority of the inhabitants.

The **Whitsun Treat** 1896 - 'To the teachers and to those who provided the tea and amusements, the best thanks are due, as also to Mr G. Smith who kindly provided the Field for the Treat, and to Mr Hook and Mr Daniells for the swings and sacks lend by them.' One can only guess at the games and fun had by the village children on this occasion.

June 1896 - A **grand Fete** in connexion with the Band of Hope will be held in the garden and grounds of Brownshill House on July 4th. 'The object is threefold: first, to provide a treat for all the members; secondly, to obtain funds to procure a piano, which is much wanted for winter entertainments; and thirdly, to interest people in the neighbourhood in the Temperance Work.' A stage was erected on the lawn and various Entertainments including a Ladies Band and the Chalford Brass Band would perform. There would also be athletic sports 'and we believe the prizes will be wonderful' The notice for this event ends with the comment: 'it is just possible that the Fete may end up with a dance' Tickets for this extravaganza cost 6d paid in advance and a maximum of 500 would be able to attend. The July edition reported: In response to predictions of wet weather 'we mean to enjoy ourselves if we have to do it mackintoshes … tickets are selling fast, but there are a few left'. There efforts were rewarded; the August edition reports that over £20 (£1,850) profit was made.

Mothers' Meeting Tea August 1896 - 'The members of our two Mothers' Meetings were entertained at the Vicarage on Tuesday afternoon … tables were set under the large walnut tree, where a substantial tea was served. After this the party adjourned to the lower lawn, to watch the struggle for the Croquet Championship which the Bussage Mothers won after an exciting game. At 6 o'clock, there was Evensong in the Parish Church, followed by more games and amusements at the Vicarage, and shortly after 8pm the pleasant afternoon came to an end.' 'Next day, the Perseverance Class enjoyed a similar treat … and on both occasions Mrs Macleod was warmly thanked for all she had done.'

Parish Library - In November 1896 a parish library was established. It seems to have been a seasonal activity, closing during the busy summer months. In the November 1900 edition, it is announced that the parish library would be re-opening on 18th November.: 'After being closed for several months … intended for the use of all Church people resident in the District … nominal Subscription of one penny a month enables Members to obtain or exchange books weekly.' The August 1902 edition of the magazine comments that 'it is gratifying to learn that the number or books taken out during the past Season shows a large increase, and that more grown-up persons now make use of the Library.' This implies that there is an increase in both literacy and the leisure time to enjoy books which would have been impossible in 1846 when the church was built. Following this accolade is a request for more books or funds to purchase the same. A further comment in June 1903, laments the fact that books are not brought back as regularly as they should!

January 1897 – a **Concert** is held in the Schoolroom – 'the best Concert ever given at Bussage' 'In the space at our disposal it is impossible to do full justice to the Entertainment … of individual performers, we put Janet Davis first. She had a good deal to do, and did it all capitally.' Other names mentioned are Gardiner Clissold, Grace Clissold and Mildred

Gardiner, Frank Hatton, Harry Hook. 'The Girls' singing deserves a word of praise. Their voices were carefully trained … the Boys' Drill was performed in good style.' Prized distributed during the interval included Mrs Macleod's Prize for Sewing won by Kate Roberts.

May 1898 – **another concert** takes place in the schoolroom: 'the chief attraction of the Concert was Mrs Macleod's Band, which gave capital renderings of Hadyn's and Romberg's 'Toy Symphonies'. The Band consisted of the following: Pianoforte, Miss Leech; Drum, Mrs Macleod; Rattle, Mrs Sibree; Triangle, Mrs Wheeler; Quail, Miss Smyth; Cuckoo, Miss Z Smyth; Nightingale, Miss Wheeler; Trumpets, Messrs Carroll and Thackwell; Bells, Mr B Carroll; with Miss Rudd as Conductor' Proceeds of concert £3 7s were given to school funds – this would be equal to £350 today.

Entertainments - Mrs Macleod continues in her efforts to raise funds for the school by providing entertainments and in January 1899, the following note appears in the Magazine: 'Reports of it [The Entertainment arranged by Mrs Macleod] have reached distant lands; one of our Foreign Correspondents, writing from Switzerland, states that it has been heard of there "as being the best which has been given in Bussage for years."' £4 (£360) was raised for the school funds.

June 1897 – Celebrations for **Queen Victoria's Diamond Jubilee:** Saturday June 19 – unveiling of the new church clock by Mrs Macleod, with a short service of dedication. On Sunday June 20 there would also be services of thanksgiving and praise.

Tuesday June 22 – A Public Dinner in the large tent on the Recreation Ground at 2.00 p.m. 'Invitation tickets will be issued by the Committee to all Parishioners of the age of 15 years and upwards.' The Chalford String Band will perform during the day. At 4.30 p.m. the Children will be entertained at Tea … and at 5.30, Sports of various kinds will begin. … It is intended to light a large Bonfire at 10.0pm' All were expected to bring their own plate, cup, knife, fork etc. The Committee would have special badges

However, the report in the July edition makes it clear that, although the weather was not good - it rained - all the same a good time was had by all. The Clock was unveiled by Mrs Macleod who said: 'This Clock is dedicated to the Glory of Almighty God, and erected in Commemoration of the 60th year of Her Majesty's Reign, for the use hereafter of the parishioners of this Parish'.

August 1897 - **Band of Hope Outing**
A party of about 70 went to Westonbirt 'the beautiful gardens belonging to Captain Holford' in 3 brakes. They left Chalford at 9.30 and got to Tetbury just before 12 noon, reaching Westonbirt around 1pm. The landlord of The Hare and Hounds at Westonbirt told them that they would be shown round the gardens at 3.30 and offered his field for games while they waited. 'A game of cricket was started for the men and boys, and the girls made for the swings,

while the mothers sat down and looked on.' On their return from the gardens, tea was laid on in a tent in the garden of the Hare and Hounds after which there were more games until 8pm when they set off for home, getting back to Chalford just before 10pm. But that was not the end of the excitement - 'Coming down Hyde Hill a pony driven by a lady coming up shied at our light and turned her over in the road almost under the horses' feet. Fortunately she was not hurt.'

August 1898- **Mothers' group Outing** which went by train to Bath where St Mary's Bathwick Church House was made available to the group for a picnic lunch, 'the use of which had been obtained through the kindly interest of an old friend of Mrs Macleod's'. This was followed by a walk around the shops, and to Victoria Park where they listened to the band. Here they were joined by Mr and Mrs Kemble 'to whom they were indebted for the use of' the Church House for tea. Then followed a trip to the Abbey. What a vast difference the accessibility of the railway made to the locality!

Choir outings:
Saturday 25 June 1898 – The men of the choir went by train to Brighton (4am from Brimscombe station), then they took the steamer to Eastbourne – the sea was rough! They got back to Bussage at 2.30 a.m. but 'long as their day had been, all felt that it had gone off well, and all were ready to take their parts in the Church services on Sunday'

August 1900 - By train again, on 6th August, the men

and boys of the choir went together to Weymouth. They left Brimscombe at 5.50 a.m. returning at 1.40 a.m. But when they arrived at Weymouth 'ominous clouds had been gathering for some time, and as the Party left the Station rain was falling in torrents, and a high wind blowing down the Esplanade … an excellent meal, however, cheered every one up, and when it was pointed out that the rain … was certainly less heavy, their spirits followed the rain's example … before long the sun was shining brightly, and if the wind blew more strongly than ever this in its way added to the amusement, for by getting into a sheltered corner and holding your hat firmly on your head, you could enjoy the fun of watching other people running wildly after theirs … most of the Party took ship for Portland [which] will be remembered for the magnificent sight presented by the sea as its waves thundered on Chessil Beach.'

August 1902 and the senior choir members went by brake at 4am to Stroud then by the 5.15 am train they proceeded to Bournemouth where they arrived at 10am. 'The party walked through the fine Public Gardens to the beach.' Some went to Swanage by boat. Others got the bus to Boscombe and walked back over the cliffs. The train left Bournemouth at 8pm, arriving at Stroud at midnight, so the party did not get back to Bussage until 1am 'not too fatigued to prevent them being in their places at the morning service.' The choirboys went on an outing to Bristol and Clifton by train where they visited St Mary Redcliffe, went shopping and ate dinner. They also enjoyed seeing the electric tram and 'the lift' at Clifton, the Suspension Bridge, then the Zoo and tea, before getting the train back.

June 1900 and the village celebrates the **Relief of Mafeking** which 'caused much local rejoicing. The Village was gay with flags, and the enthusiasm of the School Children was so great that after singing "God save the Queen" in the Playground, they marched through the Village waving flags and cheering loudly.'

Children's Flower Show - May 22nd 1902 – 'only children attending the day school may exhibit, and none but wild flowers, grasses and leaves may be used and these must be arranged by the exhibitor without any other person's help. ... the Show is, of course, an experiment, but there is no reason why it should not be successful.' Sadly, the report in the June Edition says that the weather was bad which 'seriously affected the attendance'. 'The Show itself was excellent.' Buns, oranges and lemonade were provided.

July 1902 - **Women's Guild Outing** – 'a most delightful drive, through Birdlip to Cheltenham, in Mr Kilminster's comfortable and roomy brake.' 'At Cheltenham, most of the time before and after dinner was spent in looking in at shop windows and making various purchases.' On the way back, they stopped at Birdlip for a tea (an hour and a half), getting back at 9.30pm.

July 1904 - **Sunday School Treat** for the children who marched to church for a service, then paraded back through the village with flags waving before being 'photographed by Miss Burgess' ending the occasion with the National Anthem. 'Each child presented with an orange and a bun'. Life was so much simpler then!

Welfare

Mrs Macleod worked very hard at doing what she could to improve the condition of the families of the village. One way she used was the Mothers' meeting which was held at the Vicarage every Wednesday at 2.30 p.m. This meeting was obviously well attended. It seems to have consisted of an opportunity for the mothers to sew clothing for their families with fabric provided by their hostess for which they could pay a little weekly and also included refreshment. The mums were read to while they sewed – doubtless an opportunity for a little religious education. But this would have been an important opportunity for the women to discuss matters relevant to them – the immunisation of their children, for example. The following reports in the Magazine give us a little insight into the lives of the women of the village.

November 1895 – At the Mothers' meeting held at the Vicarage a '**Boot Club**' was started 'for the benefit of Members, who will receive a bonus of a penny on every shilling'.

October 1896 - A good supply of flannel, etc, has been obtained, which will be on view at the opening meeting of this winter. 'The Boot Club will be continued as before, and will probably become more valued as it is better known.'

November 1899 - there will be the usual supplies of flannel, Holland and other useful articles at the very lowest prices. No one is obliged to work; some may prefer to sit and listen to the reading. Babies in arms are not objected to but children who run about disturbing others cannot be admitted.'

October 1900 announces the closure of the Clothing Club. 'There was a time when it proved of great value and service to many in the Parish, but this has now passed; the number of those who belong to it has diminished, and their interest in it continues to decrease. Like many an undertaking, it has fulfilled its purpose and served its end … a means of promoting regularity amongst those who availed themselves of its benefits … the Post Office Savings Bank, now established in our Village, enables all to place their weekly savings in safe deposit.' This relatively insignificant note marks a massive change in the social conditions prevalent in the village.

Christmas 1896 – but not all are better off: '**alms will be given to the Poo**r, as they were last year, when after providing ten or twelve families with Christmas dinners and coal, enough money was left to purchase a pair of warm blankets which are again on loan for the winter.' Can you imagine being so poverty-stricken that you have to borrow blankets? But at least there are blankets to be borrowed; that makes a difference.

Parish café - January 1899, 'Mrs Macleod hopes before long to be able to announce the existence of a place in Bussage where from early morning till night, cups of hot Tea, Coffee, and Cocoa, with Biscuits or Bread and Butter, can be obtained. This should be a great boon to our villagers through the winter.' This was opened in February of that year.

July 1900 - The **epidemic of measles**, which has been so prevalent in Stroud and other parts of the neighbourhood, found its way into our Village towards the end of May, and has necessitated the temporary closing of the National School. Happily there have been no serious cases and the school will have been re-opened before this appears in print.'

June 1902 - **Coal club** – a suggestion appears in the Magazine that payment of 2s to 4s a month, payable to Mrs Macleod at the vicarage on the first Monday of each month would result in 'a bonus of 2d in the shilling will be added to the payments in December' June edition reports good uptake. In December 1902, the Magazine reports that this club has been 'appreciated by those who joined' and that 'the Coal (one ton per member) was delivered'. The club will be started again in May 'with 2d in the shilling being paid by Mrs Macleod to each member who has fully paid up by the first Monday in November'. By 1904, Mrs Macleod is having to state that the club is restricted to church attendees only and is 'meant only for such as are really in need of such help, and cannot afford to pay the full price for coal in the winter.'

This situation continued until September 1904 when the Macleods left Bussage. However, the principle was continued. Mrs Macleod put the following note into the Magazine: 'the Members' payments cover the cost of the coal, bought by the truck-load, but the additional expenditure for hauling from Brimscombe Station has hitherto been paid by me. Before leaving the Parish, I should like to place this on a different footing, and therefore ask for small donations to meet this expense.'

I know I am repeating this theme time after time, but I make no apology for it - so little is ever said of the vital input of Vicar's wives to the work of the parish! The amount of work involved in the running of all these financial activities must have been colossal, not to mention the unrelenting generosity that underpinned it all.

March 1904 and mention is made of a **District Nurse** – in fact there is a collection at evensong on 20 March which is given to the District Nurses' Association in recognition of the 'great benefit of having a district Nurse amongst us'.

Missionary Work

The parish was encouraged from the start to look out beyond its borders and to support the work of the Church in other places. The fact that so many of the clergy who served in Bussage worked in the mission field and their hands-one experience must have enhanced this. The Magazine reports many activities and here are a few of them.

January 1896 – the schoolroom **hosted a lecture** on the Universities' Mission to Central Africa by Rev. H. W. Gerrish. 'Rain again fell heavily, but in spite of this, the Schoolroom was well filled.' [Rev. Gerrish died on 30 July 1897 – from fever in Zanzibar.]

March 1897 - **Plague and famine in India** – generous collection forwarded to the Mansion House (London) appeal.

Link with Lebombo
June 1897 –- The Bishop of Lebombo, son of Rev. Christopher Smyth, is to speak at a service in August. He was thanked for preaching at the Choral Celebration on 4th Sunday after Easter and 'for other assistance rendered by him during the past month'. He had, according to the October edition, been attending the Lambeth Conference. However, he also preached on 15th August and returned on 1st September. Comment is made of 'his great kindness in so often taking part in our Services, not only on occasions when he preached, but at week-day Services as well.' Obviously he was keen to keep the link with the parish where his father had worked – he would have been an ordained priest by the time his father took the incumbency.

The February 1902 Magazine contains reports of two concerts: one at the schoolroom on 13 Jan and another at the reading room on 2nd Jan. where Chalford String Band played. It was noted that the

Bishop of Lebombo 'dropped in to smoke a pipe and have a chat about his neighbours the Boers.' What a delightful image that creates!

He was not the only connection with Lebombo: On the eighth Sunday after Trinity in 1902, Rev. T. Hainsworth, Mission-Priest of the Diocese of Lebombo preached at Bussage.

The link continues, in February 1905 a talk on conditions in Lebombo is given by Miss Saunders, 'who as one of the lady workers there was able to graphically describe the ways and habits of the native children and the methods adopted by the Mission to bring them and their parents under the good influences of the Christian religion.'

March 1901 and the **Rev. Simpson**, who had been overseeing the parish while the Rev. and Mrs Macleod were in Italy for Mrs Maclean's health, left Bussage to return to Zanzibar. However, 'Owing to the wreck of the S.S. "Holland", Mr Simpson, who had forwarded his luggage by her, lost everything, books, outfit and all.' The Congregation at Bussage collected £17 to send to him. 'as a small token' of their sympathy and a thank you for all his work in the absence of the Vicar.

May 1901 reports the death of **Rev. Henry Jacobs**, yet another of the missionaries whose foundations in the faith had been laid in Bussage: 'the late Dean's clerical work began in Bussage, to which he was ordained Deacon in 1847, very shortly after the Church was consecrated.' Jacobs worked in New

Zealand for 50 years.

Behaviour Issues

November 1985 - **Segregated seating in Church**
'At a fully-attended Meeting of the Churchwardens and Sidesmen … the following Resolution was adopted unanimously:- that on Sunday Evenings, the Seats in the Parish Church shall be allotted thus:- South and Side Aisles – for Men and Boys; North Aisle and West End – for Women and Girls'. However, in September 1897 it is reported that the privilege of not observing this on Sunday mornings 'has recently been taken advantage of by others and the Vicar hopes that the mention of the fact will suffice to prevent the repetition of the annoyance referred to'. Thanks were subsequently extended to the congregation for their assistance in carrying out the Resolution adopted at the Special Meeting of the Vestry on 22nd. Without their aid, it would have been difficult to enforce the new Regulation …the few unruly spirits were speedily shown that the intention was to carry it out thoroughly. It is gratifying to hear so many expressions of approval of the change … a decisive check has been given to the unseemly behaviour which was formerly so noticeable.' What this unseemly behaviour comprised, we do not know, but reference to Samuel Pepys diary entries written a mere 200 years previously, where he describes how he tried to put his hand up the skirt of the lady beside him perhaps gives an indication of the sort of behaviour that could

take place. I might add that the lady in question resorted to sticking pins in the diarist to stop him.

March 1896 sees a reminder that the Bye-laws for the Good Rule and Government of the Administrative County of Gloucester state "No person shall in any street or public place wilfully and persistently loiter or smoke at or near the entrance of any Church, during the time of Divine Service, or during the assembly thereat or departure therefrom of the congregation, in such a manner as to cause annoyance to persons going to, attending at, or returning from any such place of worship."

November 1896 - 'the objectionable habit of loafing about the Church-yard gate before Service on Sunday Evenings has not been got rid of yet. Several persons have lately been annoyed by the men and lads who collect there and almost block up the pathway … who think it fun to annoy ladies and insult young women.'

November 1897 - A Magic Lantern Entertainment – a tour of the Engadine was spoiled by bad behaviour. 'Serious complaints have reached us of the ill-mannered behaviour of some of the lads at the back of the room whilst the Magic Lantern was shown.' Offenders will be refused entry in future.

December 1987 - 'The Hassocks supplied in Church are meant to kneel upon, not to serve as boot-scrapers, as some of the Congregation appear to think.'

1898 - In the March edition, there is a note: 'Dirty boots account for much untidiness. … there is a foot-scraper on either side of the Porch' it appears people are treading a lot of mess into the Church. There is also a note complaining that the notices requesting kneeling pads be replaced after use have been torn down – it is concluded that this must be children's work and parents are requested to curb their behaviour.

There is also yet another reminder of the fact that it is illegal to loiter outside a church during divine service and that the penalty is a fine of up to 40s. Obviously there is still a problem with this.

June 1899 - Flowers are being stolen from graves. Macleod quotes how the grave of Bishop Mackenzie 'who died and is buried in a distant part of Central Africa … [the grave] is carefully kept and tended by the untaught, unchristianized natives … There the grave of a stranger is respected and cared for, here, the graves of our own people are robbed and spoiled …' The July edition reports 'further thefts from the Churchyard have to be chronicled … roses were on two occasions stolen off the trees … the matter has been placed in the hands of the District Superintendent of police' It seems that this is a problem in the local area. It is thought children are doing it and parents are called to 'see that their children are brought up to regard with reverence all that has to do with Church and Churchyard.'

July 1900 – But a year later and it still goes on - 'All who love our Church and its surroundings, and desire to prevent desecration, are invited to assist in putting a stop to the mean and despicable practice of stealing roses from the Churchyard. The Vicar and Churchwardens are determined to prosecute any person found committing theft.'

October 1900 - 'The unseemly behaviour of some who came to Church on the evening of the day of our Harvest Thanksgiving is a matter for deep regret.' There followed a recognition that the troublemakers were not regular attendees and a polemic on standards of behaviour in church generally.

February 1901 - 'we are glad our sidesmen have at last asserted their authority. The quietness and good behaviour of the young men who sit in the aisle on Sunday Evenings is now delightful to see.' What exactly was going on prior to this remains a secret! I can't help but envisage the sidesmen with large sticks … doubtless a totally false image.

June 1901 and following extract is published in the parish magazine in an effort to curb bad behaviour by targeting the mothers: **Morality in the village**
'Every married woman's duty is to keep her house clean and respectable, and a proper resting-place for her husband when he comes in from work, so that he may not be driven to seek rest and refreshment elsewhere.' Regarding children - 'are you, Mothers, setting them a good example' 'Your girls fritter their money in finery, instead of getting useful lasting clothes, in order to attract the attention of some brainless youth; later on, they walk out with him, and you allow it'. 'A man, when drunk, is no better than

a lunatic – yes, *a lunatic*, only worse; for he has brought it upon himself by doing what even a dog will not do. If there were less drunkenness in this Village, there would be happier homes and more regular worshippers in our little Church.'

March 1903 – the parishioners are reminded (once again) that a Gloucester By-law states: 'no person shall in any street or public place wilfully and persistently loiter or smoke at or near the entrance to any church, Chapel, Meeting-house or other place of worship during the time of Divine service, or during the assembly thereat or departure therefrom of the congregation, in such manner as to cause annoyance to persons going to, attending at, or returning from any such places of worship.' Obviously there was an ongoing problem, though probably not caused by the people who actually read the magazine!

April 1903 and the situation has clearly deteriorated as the following note appears in the magazine: 'the recent injury to our Parish Clerk calls renewed attention to the danger of stone-throwing. It is of comparatively little use for the School Teachers to warn the children ... unless parents correct and punish those who offend, and the lads learn to control themselves.' Anyone found throwing stones and causing injury or annoyance will be liable to a fine of 40s under local by-laws.

Church

June 1896 - 'Few English villages enjoy, as ours does, the privilege and blessing of a Confirmation Service every year; in other places Candidates frequently have to journey to a Church at some distance off. Owning to our Bishop's kindly interest in Bussage, no such inconvenience is felt here, so that we have good cause for thankfulness.'

September 1896 - **Patronal Festival**
Rev. Henry Arnott 'had promised to preach to us on that day' but he had an accident and could not appear. In the November edition it says: 'nothing equalled the effect produced at the Celebration of the Holy Eucharist on St. Michael's Day, attended as it was by so strikingly large a congregation and accompanied by the full Ritual of the Catholic Church ... that such Services are possible in an English village Church on ordinary working-days is a true cause for joy and thankfulness.' He goes on to extend thanks to the ladies who decorated the church. 'Nor must we omit to thank our Organist and the members of our Choir ... [but] if we may venture on a criticism, we should say that the chief thing required of them is ... the harmonious blending of the several voices and not on the prominence of any single voice. The singing would be all the better if it were less loud'

Harvest - 20th September 1896 'not only has the Wheat Harvest been good, as it has been throughout England, but the Hay Crop was by no means poor, which it was in many other parts.' This comment is followed by a request that donations 'when sent in any quantity, were to be placed in baskets and arranged with flowers or ferns, that they would not only be more suitably arranged in Church but also be more conveniently sent to the poor and sick'. September edition comments thus: 'The Church looked very beautiful on Sunday … the resemblance to an over-stocked greengrocer's shop, which we have seen in other Churches, was happily wanting'.

October 1896 – the 50th **anniversary of consecration of church** – 'is it likely that the first Vicar, the dearly-love Robert Alfred Suckling, has forgotten the Church he held so dear? or that Edmund Nelson Dean, whose last earthly resting-place is beneath its walls, has forgotten it?' In his sermon that night, the Vicar referred to some striking changes there have been in this district … since 1837, the year of the Queen's Accession. During this period, three parish churches have been built, at Oakridge, Bussage and France Lynch; at Bisley the Church has been restored, and the church at Chalford much enlarged. The Vicarage at Bisley has been almost rebuilt, and new Vicarages have been built in the other four places; whilst Schools have been supplied in every one of these places, and Eastcombe also, by the Church's means. All this achieved as a result of the self-sacrifice of the Oxford Twenty.

March 1897 - 'It is generally supposed that week-day congregations are composed of Women, and that without them Churches might be closed. Doubtless this is often the case, but amongst ourselves the relative position of the sexes has been reversed of late. On more than one Friday evening, the members of the Choir have outnumbered the occupants of the

Women's seats'

May 1897 **Finances** – A Vestry meeting is informed that the Church debt amounts to £26 7s 10 ½d (£2,300 today)… 'The Vicar alone is out of pocket.' He comments: 'I remember being told shortly after coming here by one of my Parishioners, that he did not call Bussage a "Living", he called it a "Starving". The recent increase in costs which has caused this deficit has been due to necessary cleaning and heating - 'It has been said: "Go to Bussage Church to a week-day Service in Lent or Advent, and send for the doctor when you get home!" meaning to go to Church was a sure way to catch a chill.'

June 1897 - '**Queen Victoria Clergy Sustenation Fund**' – 'the object of which is to increase the present miserably small incomes of the Parish Clergy. The claims of this Fund have been strongly urged by our Bishop, who lately called attention to the fact that in the Diocese of Gloucester and Bristol fully 72 livings are under £100 a year (Bussage being one of them) and there are 148 or more which do not reach £200 a year.'

March 1899 – **Church Ritual Issues** 'The Bishop has written to the Vicar asking him to arrange that at every Celebration of the Holy Communion the requisite number should communicate with the Priest. Whilst the Vicar cannot compel people to communicate late, and would regret causing any to depart from the accustomed and pious custom of receiving the Blessed Sacrament before other food, yet at the same time he is very anxious that the

Bishop's wishes should be complied with.'

'In order to more fully comply with the Prayer Book rule and the Bishop's requirements, it has been thought advisable to discontinue for the present the Monday Celebration of the Holy Eucharist. … In order that the further Prayer Book requirement of daily Mattins may be said at a time convenient to the Congregation, this Service will in future be said in Church on Monday mornings at 10.0 o'clock.'

'When so much is being said and written about the "Rules of the Prayer Book", and the (supposed) 'Disobedience' of a section of the Clergy to such Rules, it is not out of place to call attention to one of these Prayer Book Rules which is binding on the Laity.' (attendance at least 3 times a year of which Easter must be one).

April 1899 - **Dissent in the land**
'…at a time like the present it is expedient that all should rally round the Church … in a parish not far from Stroud, a Nonconformist was elected Church Warden … owing to the apathy of the Church members.' There is much concern about what is going on in churches and English Church Union was formed to clarify 'the Duty of Churchmen under the present distress'. The intention of the Union is: 'to defend and maintain unimpaired the Doctrine and Discipline of the Church against all assaults, whether from Erastianism, Rationalism, or Puritanism, from within, or from the efforts of Roman Controversialists and others from without.' 'The recent persistent and bitter and, at times,

unscrupulous attacks on the Doctrine and Worship of the Church by Sir William Harcourt[62], Lord Grimthorpe, Mr Kensit[63], and others, have induced many to join who previously held aloof'.

Having explained this, Macleod issued a plea for all Parishioners to attend the Vestry meeting. 'Urgent – We learn that a determined effort is to be made to oust the Parishioners' Warden, whose valuable services are known to all. … Every effort then should be made by us, for although there is no doubt that the great majority of our Parishioners are perfectly satisfied with things as they are, yet any apathy or indifference on their part may be the means of allowing a small, but active minority to do incalculable harm, and spread bitterness and discord

---

[62] *A great parliamentary debater, he sprinkled his speeches with humour. From 1898 to 1900 he was conspicuous, both on the platform and in letters to The Times, in demanding active measures against* **Ritualism in the Church of England***. However, his attitude in this was reflected in his political advocacy of* **disestablishment***.*

[63] *The ecclesiastical agitation of 1898, 1899, and 1900, caused by the growth of ritualism, gave Kensit his opportunity. He now organised a band of itinerant young preachers, named 'Wicliffites,' who created disturbances in ritualistic churches throughout the country. In January 1897 he first attained general notoriety by publicly objecting in the church of St. Mary-le-Bow to the confirmation of Mandell Creighton [q. v. Suppl. I] as bishop of London. Early in 1898 he began an organised anti-ritualist campaign in London. Selecting St. Ethelburga's, Bishopsgate, as the object of an attack, he qualified himself by residence as a parishioner, and frequently interrupted the services. On Good Friday 1898 he protested against the adoration of the cross at St Cuthbert's, Philbeach Gardens. He was fined 3l. for brawling in church, but was acquitted on appeal to the Clerkenwell quarter sessions. Bishop Creighton forbade the extreme practices to which Kensit objected, but disregarded his threats of further interference. In the same year at the Bradford church congress Kensit denounced the bishop's weakness.*

---

throughout the Parish.'

The vestry meeting was the largest ever held – nearly 70 people present of whom 50% were rate payers (and therefore eligible to vote). Mr Samuel Wallis was re-elected as Parishioners' Warden with none standing against him. Then a vote of thanks for all the work done by the wardens (Wallis and Hook) was proposed and there was one dissentor! Macleod comments: 'It might have been supposed that after the Church Officials had been unanimously re-appointed, no one would have grudged offering them thanks, but human nature, under certain conditions, is strangely illogical.'

The problems continued into June: the English Church Union – meeting reports that the Union has been accused of 'treason and treachery so publicly and lavishly'. Mention is made of 'those two great admissions of Mr Balfour, viz., the claim of the Church of England to be the great Catholic Church, and also her right to self-government. If that venomous Bill to be brought forward by Mr Austin Taylor should become law, it would reduce the Church to a mere State department' (the Bill was rejected by a majority of 2-1 in the Commons) 'It was the aim of the State to control the laity, the discipline, the faith and doctrine of the Church'.

February 1901 **Damage to the Church Building** 'Strong gales in January damaged the roof ... and the rain made its way through.' Part of the boundary wall has since fallen owing to the heavy rains. Churchwardens repaired the roof and will see to the wall when the weather improves. Rains caused a landslip between the Vicarage and Eastcombe. 'Fortunately the greatest movement took place where there were no houses, but the effect was felt as far as the Glebe land, where it caused serious damage to the private road, whilst further on a slight settlement took place in the gable end of the Stable.'

Bible Classes – Rev. Hayward took up his post in January 1904 and was obviously not going to let the grass grow under his feet and by April the announcement is made in the magazine that a men's Bible class has started. They are studying Acts 18. The following month he starts a Sunday afternoon class for those lads too old for Sunday school but not yet men and takes over the running of the choir which used to be organised by the school head teacher but he has moved on. They have three practices a week. However, the young women are not to be left out as Mrs Hayward and Miss Fuller set up a class and, after taking tea, they played hand football!

Social Change

On 1st May 1896 the Bussage Post Office opened. 'This is due to representations made by the Vicar (Macleod) to the Postal Authorities.' By June, it is reported that 'the Postal Authorities are beginning to recognise Bussage as an Important place … we hear of enquiries being made with a view to opening a Telegraph Office. The September edition goes on to report that a large number of accounts have been opened since the Savings Bank was opened. March 1989 - 'An improvement in our Postal Service deserves to be chronicled. Letters, which otherwise would not be delivered until the following morning, can now be obtained on applying at the Bussage Post Office between 5.0 p.m. and 7.0 p.m.'

October 1897 - Chalford railway station has opened – this must have opened up transport possibilities to the local population as the various outings illustrate. There is an idea of moving Brimscombe station nearer to Stroud though this is unlikely to be done.

October 1899 - 'It is hoped that a **Reading and Recreation Room** may be provided for our Men and Lads during the Winter months.' 'A preliminary meeting … took place on Monday September 25th … it is hoped the Rooms may be in working order by the third week of October.' The recreation room opened on 16 October with 30 members. It is open three nights a week – Monday, Wednesday & Friday from 7.30 to 9.30. January 1900 edition speaks of : 'considerable interest was aroused by the Bagatelle, Draughts, and Dominoes Tournaments. April 1900 – the Room 'will be closed for the Season on Thursday, April 5th. Latterly, the attendance has fallen off considerably, and now that lighter evenings are approaching, the Committee think it needless to keep the Room open any longer'. The room re-opened in October; 'Men of 16 years of age and upwards are eligible as Members' in the hope that 'an evening spent there in games or reading is far more profitable than one spent in a Public House or in loafing about corners'. It is highly noticeable that no provision is made or deemed necessary to be made for the young women of the village.

December 1899 – **Boer War** - Mrs Macleod has collected £4 11s 6d (£350) for the Soldiers' and Sailors' Families Assoc. (Stroud Division) in connection with the Transvaal War – there was also a Drawing-Room Meeting at the vicarage, speaker: Rev H E Sawyer on 'The Boer as I knew him' By January 1901 'the Shadow of War … hung heavily and darkly, so that the earlier weeks of the closing year of the 19th century were full of the uttermost of sadness and gloom; now … light is shining, for the near hope of victory has replaced the year of defeat. But the Shadow has not yet cleared away; the soldiers who left our village have not yet returned home.' July 1902 and the end of the Boer war is celebrated with services of thanksgiving. The magazine announces that 'Our Reservists may now be expected home shortly, and we earnestly appeal to their friends to refrain from pressing intoxicating drink on them, but rather to help them to be as sober and manly in time of Peace as they have been in time of War..' Godfrey Davis and William Winston returned on 7 September.

November 1901 – A **girls' singing class** is to start under the auspices of Miss Sawyer and Miss Rudd. It is intended for those who work during the day. This club continued until November 1903 when arrangements were made for a fortnightly social club. Again Miss Rudd was organising it. The club opened on 17 November and was great success. A note in December edition states that 'the Men's Club flourishes; and ... so does that of 'the Gentler Sex'. It appears that the sexes are still segregated.

February 1901 **The Death of Queen Victoria**. 'Once more the tolling of the Church bell has brought home to us a sense of a terrible loss ... this whole nation is stricken with grief, for our Queen is dead.' A national day of mourning is declared for 2nd February (reported in the March edition) and an account of the service held at a church in San Remo Italy in recognition of that fact. A wreath was sent to line the route of the Funeral Procession: 'A last Tribute of Loyalty from two Hamlets on the Cotwolds to a Great Queen, Bussage, Brownshill'. The wreath was composed of laurel, lignum vitae and other evergreens relieved by golden leaves of the croton plant, chosen and put together by Miss Pidcock.

September 1901 - The population of the Ecclesiastical parish of Bussage according to the census is 296. Ten years previously it had been 315; a substantial reduction in so small a community.

April 1902 and the **Deceased Wife's Sister Bill** is the hot topic in the country. The magazine contains a diatribe against this – as being against God's law. A petition was got up in the village in April claiming that 'were it allowed to become Law, the result would be disastrous.' The May edition reports 50 signatories and 'as these were obtained without canvassing, the result is distinctly satisfactory.' At the annual meeting of the English Church Union on

5th June, a resolution was passed against this bill. The bill was defeated this time although it was passed in 1907.

Coronation of Edward VII – The coronation was due to be held on June 26 with a service at 12 noon, a public dinner at 2pm in a tent on the recreation ground for all over 15 years of age and tea for children at 4.30pm in the tent – adults can attend this if they prefer it to the dinner. However, 'adults are expected to bring with them plates, knives, forks, etc. for their own use, and that the children must bring their cups and mugs.' Dinner will also be sent to those too infirm to attend. Chalford String Band will play and there will be dancing and sports.

However, the coronation was delayed due to the king's illness. But the dinner and tea, in common with all other events planned countrywide, went ahead as it was 'the King's earnest and publicly expressed desire that the celebrations ... should be held as already arranged.'

Coronation medals were issued. These showed 'life-like portraits of Their Majesties' on one side and on the reverse 'Britannia holding aloft the Imperial Crown, and hastening towards Westminster Abbey ... accompanied by her Colonies, which are represented as children attired in their native costumes.'

The actual coronation was held 9th August. In Bussage, a service was held in the church at 2.30 p.m. at which the Chalford String Band participated in the music. The music concerned was 'known as the "Archbiship of Capetown's" and had been personally authorised by the Bishop of the Diocese for use in the Church. The congregation were issued with copies of the music and encouraged to take them away as a memento of the occasion. This was followed by tea and more music from the Band as well as sports (with prizes) and dancing at the recreation ground. The Coronation medals were presented to the children at this event.

June 1904 – Prayer is offered for the **Church of Japan** in connection with the Russian/Japanese war. A conflict overshadowed in our minds by the later cataclysmic First World War.

Humour and Oddities

'On at least two occasions we have heard it said that our Magazine is 'well worth sixpence'. We fully believe it, and … the Editors are willing to receive the additional fivepence at the Magazine Office.' Did they get it? Foolish question! November 1895

Missing teaspoons – two spoons 'engraved with the letter 'S'' were lost at the Parish Tea. February 1896

Bussage earthquake 1896: Thursday, 17 December - Macleod wrote to The Times: 'I was roused from sleep by a rumbling noise and felt ten or twelve distinct vibrations, which were followed an instant or so later by a quivering of the earth. The movement seemed to travel from north-west or west-north-west to south-west … and the china etc in the room was much disturbed. As the movement passed away, the dog chained in my stable-yard barked violently. A lady living about five-eighths of a mile south gives the hour of the shock as about 5.40 a.m. At Stroud … it was felt stronger. Earthquakes have been known here previously, though none as severe are remembered.' At the Communion held on that day, and on the following Sunday, 'thanks were offered to God for deliverance from peril and danger'

'too large a proportion of our Congregation allow the Offertory-bag to pass by them unsupported' complains a note in the March 1898 edition.

October 1900 - 'Advice to those who seek Humility: become the editor of a Parish Magazine … for you will quickly find that your longest and most favoured Articles have been left unread, whilst your pithy "Short Notes" have failed to leave any abiding impression. … The above remark is made candidly, and without bitterness. It deals with a phase of human nature which we naturally regret, but which is too universal to permit of personal feeling.' I am sure the editor of any church magazine would echo this plaintive comment.

Bussage church – postcard 1917

APPENDIX 1 – *BISHOPS, PRIESTS AND DEACONS*

Tract by 'Richard Nelson' aka Rev. Thomas Keble

Dec. 4, 1833.]
[*No.* 12—*Price* 3d.

RICHARD NELSON.

I.

————————

"It is evident unto all men *diligently* reading the Holy Scripture and ancient authors, that from the Apostles' time there have been these orders of Ministers in Christ's Church; Bishops, Priests, and Deacons."

Pref. to the Ordination Service.

IN the course of this last summer of 1833, I had the pleasure of a visit from an old and valued friend, one of the most respectable merchants in the city of Bristol, (and this, in my opinion, is no small praise.)

We were discussing one day the subject of National Schools, their merits and demerits. He was pleading strenuously for them; and to confirm his arguments, "I will mention," said he, "a circumstance which happened to me when I was in this part of the world about eleven or twelve years ago. I was travelling on a coach somewhere between Sheffield and Leeds, when we took up a lad of fourteen or fifteen years of age; a rough country-looking boy, but well mannered and of an intelligent countenance.

"I found upon conversation with him, that he belonged to a National School in the neighbourhood, which he was, he said, on the point of leaving. This gave me occasion to ask him various questions, which he answered with so much readiness and vivacity, yet without any self-conceit in his manner, that when the coach stopped (I think it was at Barnsley) for a short time, I took him with me into a bookseller's shop, and desired him to select some book which I might give him as a testimony of my approbation. After looking at a few which the bookseller recommended, he fixed on a "Selection from Bishop Wilson's Works," whose name, he said, he had often heard. He begged me to write his name in it, which I did, and we parted with mutual expressions of good-will; and I will be bold to prophesy that that boy (or young man as he must now be, if he is still alive) is giving by his conduct stronger testimony in favour of the National School System than a thousand of your speculating philosophers can bring against it."

"Well," said I, "you are apt to be sanguine in your views, but as I must confess they are very often right, so I will hope you may not have been deceived in this instance."

It so happened that two or three days after this conversation we were taking a walk together, and discussing various topics, such as the present state of things might well suggest, when we met a young man, a neighbour of mine, a mason, who detained us two or three minutes, while he asked my directions about some work he was doing for me.

After he was out of hearing,—"That," said I, "is one of the most respectable young men I know. Soon after I came here, more than four years ago, he married a young woman of a disposition similar to his own; and they live in that cottage that you see there, to the right of that row of beeches."

"I see it, I believe," said he, hardly looking the way I pointed, and not altogether seeming pleased at having our conversation thus interrupted.

"He has two or three little children, and I believe sometimes it goes hard with them, as in the winter work is short hereabouts, and he does not like beating about far from home. I sometimes tell him he ought to look farther; but he is so fond of his home, his wife and children, that I verily think he would rather live on potatoes seven days in the week with them, than have meat and beer by himself. And besides, I know he does not relish the companions he must work with at the town. However, on the whole, they do tolerably well, as they have a garden of a fair size, and he never spends an unnecessary penny."

"I am glad to hear it," said he; "but we were talking about the value of an apostolical succession in the ministry, were we not? and of the great ignorance and neglect now prevailing on the subject."

"We were," said I; "but to tell you the truth, though I have bestowed considerable attention on the subject, and examined the various opinions which have been put forth on it, yet I have scarcely learned so much hereon from the works of learned theologians, as I have from repeated conversations with that very young man we just now met."

"You surprise me," said he.

"You may be surprised, but it is however true, and, (if you have no objection,) I will tell you how it was."

"By all means," he answered.

"When I first came to the parish I looked about for some person to take charge of the Sunday School, as the master was old, and so deaf as to be unequal to the work. I was recommended to apply to Richard Nelson, (that is the man's name,")—Here my friend interrupted me, saying, "Richard Nelson? why, now I remember, that was the very name of the boy I travelled with." "Indeed!" said I, "then doubtless it is the same person: for his age will agree with your account very well, and I know he was bred at —— National School." "Well," said he, "I am quite delighted to find myself a true prophet in this instance." "Perhaps," said I, "you will be still more pleased, when you have heard all I have to tell you: you will find that your little present was by no means thrown away." "Go on," said he, "I am all attention."

"I was telling you, I believe, that I requested Nelson to become master of the Sunday School. After some little hesitation, he declined my offer, under the plea that he could not give constant and regular attendance; though he was willing to attend occasionally, and render what assistance he could. So it was arranged that the old master should still remain; and I afterwards discoverd that an unwillingness to deprive him of the little emolument, was Nelson's real reason for declining my offer. As the Sunday School is nearly three-quarters of a mile from my house, in a direction beyond Nelson's, along the Beech Walk, as we call it, it frequently happened that we joined in company as we went to and fro. We generally talked over such subjects as had reference to the School, or to the state of religion in general: and, amongst other topics, that on which you and I are conversing,—the authority of Christian ministers. I remember it was on the following occasion that the subject was started between us. I thought that I had observed one Sunday, that he was making the boys of his class, (our School professes to be on the Bell System,) that he was, I say, making his boys read the nineteenth and some other of the Thirty-nine Articles relating to the ministerial office: and that afterwards he was explaining and illustrating them, after his usual manner, by referring them to suitable parts of Scripture. On our walk homewards, I enquired if I was right in my conjecture. He said, Yes: and that, in the present state of things, he could not help thinking it quite a duty to direct the minds of young persons to such subjects. And on this and many subsequent occasions, he set forth his opinions on the matter, which I will state to you, as far as I can remember, in his own words.

"My good mother," he said, "not long before her death, which happened about half-a-year before I came to live here, said to me very earnestly one day, as I was sitting by her bed side.—'My dear Richard, observe my words: never dare to trifle with GOD ALMIGHTY.' By this I understood her to mean, that in all religious actions we ought to be very *awful,* and to seek nothing but what is right and true. And I knew that she had always disapproved of peoples' saying, as they commonly do, 'that it little matters what a man's religion is, if he is but sincere;' and 'that one opinion or one place of worship is as good as another.' To say, or think, or act so, she used to call 'Trifling with GOD's truth:' and do you not think, sir, (addressing himself to me,) that she was right?"

"Indeed I do," said I.

"And," he said, "I was much confirmed in these opinions by constantly reading a very wise, and, as I may say to you, precious book, which a gentleman gave me some years ago, whom I met by chance when I was going to see my father in the infirmary. It is called a Selection from Bishop Wilson's Works, and there are many places in it which shew what his opinions were on this subject; and I suppose, sir, there can be no doubt that Bishop Wilson was a man of extraordinary judgment and piety."

"He has ever been considered so," I answered.

"I could not think much of any one's judgment or piety either, who should say otherwise," he replied; "and what Bishop Wilson says, is this, or to this effect:—That 'to reject the government of Bishops, is to reject an ordinance of God.'"[1]

That "our salvation depends, under God, upon the ministry of those whom JESUS CHRIST and the HOLY GHOST have appointed to reconcile men to God."[2]

That "the personal failings of ministers do not make void their commission."[3]

That "if the Unity of the Church is once made a light matter, and he who is the centre of Unity, and in CHRIST's stead, shall come to be despised, and his authority set at nought, then will error and infidelity get ground; JESUS CHRIST and His Gospel will be despised, and the kingdom of Satan set up again here as well as in other nations."[4] With many other expressions like these.

"And yet, Sir," he continued, "the gentleman who lives over there, (pointing to a great house in sight four or five miles off down the valley,) who is said to be a person of much learning, and who does a great deal of good, he does not take the matter in the same light. For he told a man of——whom I was working with, that if a person preached what was right and good, that was the best sign of his being ordained a minister, without the ceremony of laying on a Bishop's hands upon his head. And the man that told me, very much admired the opinion, in regard (he said) of its being so very *liberal,* or some such word. Though I confess I could not exactly see what there was so much to admire. Because, if the opinion were true, it was good, and if it were false, it was bad, equally as much (to my thinking) whether it were called liberal or bigotted."

"Doubtless you were right," said I. "And," he proceeded, "it seemed to me, (and I told the man so,) like going round and round in a wheel, to say. If he is GOD's minister, he preaches what is good; and if he preaches what is good, he is GOD's minister. For still the question will be, what *is* right and good? and some would say one thing and some another; and some would say there is nothing right nor good at all in itself, but only as seems most expedient to every person for the time being. So for my own satisfaction, and hoping for God's blessing on my endeavour, I resolved to search the matter out for myself as well as *I* could. My plan was this. First, to see what was said on the subject in the Church Prayer Book, and then to compare this with the Scriptures; and if, after all, I could not satisfy myself, I should have taken the liberty of consulting you, Sir, if I had been here, or Mr. ——, who was the minister at ——, where I came from."

"Yours was a good plan," I said; "but I suppose you had forgotten that the chief part of the Church Services which relate to these subjects, is not contained in the Prayer Books which we commonly use."

"I was aware of that," he answered, "but my wife's father had been clerk of —— parish, and it so happened that the churchwarden had given him a large Prayer Book in which all the Ordination Services were quite perfect, though the book was ancient, and in some parts very ragged. This book my wife brought with her when we came here, and indeed she values it very highly on account of her poor father having used it for so many years. Thus you see, Sir, with the Bible and Prayer Book, and, (as I hoped,) GOD's blessing on my labours, I was not, as you may say, unfurnished for the work."

"Indeed, Richard, you were not," I replied.

"Well then," he proceeded, "I first observed, that the church is very particular in not allowing any administration of the Sacraments, or any *public* service of ALMIGHTY GOD to take place, except when there is one of her Ministers to guide and take the lead in the solemnity. Thus not only in the administration of Baptism, and of the Lord's Supper, but in the daily Morning and Evening Prayers, in the Public Catechizing of Children, in the Solemnization of Marriage, in the Visitation of the Sick, and in the Burial of the Dead;—in all these cases the Christian congregation is never supposed complete, nor the service perfect, unless there be also present a minister authorized to lead the devotions of the people. And yet I also observed that neither minister nor people, not even with the leave of the Bishop himself, had power or authority given them to alter or vary from the Rules set down in the Prayer Book. And often have I thought how well it would be if Ministers and people too would be more careful to keep to the rules."

"Yes," said I, "it is too true; we are all to blame."

"But," he proceeded, taking a small Prayer Book out of his pocket, "the question I had next to ask was,— who are meant by these Ministers so often referred to in the Church Service. To this question I found a general answer in the Twenty-third, Twenty-sixth, and Thirty-sixth Articles; where the judgment of the Church is thus plainly given:—

1st. "That it is not lawful for any man to take upon him the office of public preaching, or ministering the Sacraments in the Congregation, before he be lawfully called and sent to execute the same."

2ndly. "That those *are* lawfully called and sent, who are chosen and called to the work by men who have public authority given them in the Congregation to call and send Ministers into the Lord's vineyard."

3rdly. "That though sometimes evil men may have chief authority in the ministration of the Word and Sacraments; yet, forasmuch, as they do not the same in their own name but in Christ's, and do minister by His commission and authority, we may use their ministry with full hope of God's blessing."

4thly. "That whosoever are consecrated and ordained according to the Rites there prescribed, are rightly, orderly, and lawfully consecrated and ordained."

"But here. Sir, I will take occasion to ask you whether it would not have been better, instead of calling the second order of Ministers Priests, to have used the word which is frequently found in the New Testament applied to them, "Elders," or "Presbyters."

"Why," I said, "I have no doubt the wise and good men who framed the Prayer Book had a good reason for retaining the title of Priests. But in truth it is one of the very words you mentioned, only somewhat shortened by our forefathers in their pronunciation of it—Presbyter was made Prester, and that by degrees became Prest, or Priest."

"That," said he "is very remarkable, and proves that we ought to enquire before we find fault. But to go on with what I was saying—I next proceeded to read over, and I assure you, Sir, I did it with great care, the three Services in our Great Prayer Book— namely, for Consecration of Bishops, Ordaining of

Priests, and Making of Deacons. And I must confess to you that I could not but greatly admire them; and at the same time feel much astonishment at two considerations which they brought to my mind."

"What were they, Richard?" I enquired.

"The one was," he said, "to think that after such a solemn dedication to the ministry, there should be such a thing as a careless or a wicked Clergyman. And yet, Sir, is it not also astonishing that after such a solemn dedication of ourselves as we all make to GOD in Baptism, there should be such a thing as a careless or a wicked Christian?"

"So it is," I said, "when we judge others we condemn ourselves. But what was the other ground of your surprise?"

"Why, it was this; that there should be any doubt what the opinion of the Church is respecting the Christian Ministry. Comparing the Ordination Service with the Liturgy and Articles, it seems to me quite clear, that in the judgment of the Church, none can shew themselves duly authorized Ministers of Christ, who do not belong to one or other of the three orders, of Bishops, Priests, or Deacons.

"But, said I to myself, other Churches have erred, why may not this then be the misfortune of the Church of England also? and this very opinion may be one of her errors. You see then, Sir, the next thing I had to do was to consult the Scriptures on the subject, and (if it be not too bold in such a one as I to say so) to try the Prayer Book by the Bible."

"Your method was the best possible," I said. "But, if you please, do not use the expression, the Church *of* England, but the Church *in* England."

"Why indeed, Sir," said he, "in the present state of things perhaps it would be more proper. But to proceed with my enquiry. I first observed, that in the History of the Jews, as contained in the Old Testament, as well as in that of Christians in the New, the ALMIGHTY seems almost or quite always to have communicated His will to mankind through some chosen Minister; some one, whether it were angel or man, who could give suitable evidence of the authority by which he spoke or acted. But there seemed to me to be this great difference between Jews and Christians, in this as in other cases; that in the Jews' religion, all the rules and regulations were set down so plainly and distinctly, that no one could mistake their meaning; for instance, in the Levitical laws concerning the priesthood; of what family and tribe the Priests and High Priest should be, what their respective duties, and what their dress, &c. Whereas in the Christian religion, the rules and regulations, however important, and even necessary, are yet not so exactly set down. And I remember hearing a very good and wise Clergyman say in a Sermon at —— Church, that this is probably what St James means, when he calls the Gospel 'a Law of Liberty;' namely, that its rules and directions are *not* so plainly set down, *on purpose,* that Christians might have freer space, (I remember that was his expression,) and opportunity, to exercise their Faith and Love for their Redeemer. And I have sometimes thought myself, that what St. Paul says about the difference between walking by faith and by sight, seems to suit the different cases of Jews and Christians. *They* walked by sight, we must walk by faith; and faith, in this world, we are told, can see but as through a glass darkly."

"It seems, so," I said.

He proceeded.

"With this view I went on to examine the New Testament, expecting to find therein some *general* instruction respecting the institution and authority of Ministers in the Christian Church. But I did not expect that these rules should be as particular and distinct as those on the same subject in the Old Testament, any more than I should expect to find a command to Christians to observe the LORD's Day set down as distinctly as the command to observe the Sabbath was set down for the Jews. And yet, Sir, I suppose all will agree, that no one who wilfully neglects the LORD's Day can be a true Christian."

"There are strange opinions now afloat," said I; "and if many despise the LORD's Ministers, it is no wonder if many also despise the LORD's Day.

"Indeed, Sir," said he, "it is not to be wondered at. But to go on with my statement. On carefully perusing the New Testament History, I remarked that our LORD did not grant ministerial authority to His disciples in general, but first to twelve, and then to seventy; that of those twelve, one was among the wickedest of mankind, and that our Lord knew (St. John vi. 64. xiii. 18.) his character when he appointed him; that possibly some of those seventy also might be unworthy persons; that our LORD, just before His departure, gave what may be called a fresh commission to His Apostles, which they should act upon after His ascension; that after that event, the twelve Apostles were the leading persons in the Christian Church, having under them two orders or degrees, viz. Bishops (sometimes called Elders) and Deacons; that this threefold division of Ministers in the Church lasted as far as the New Testament History reaches, the Apostles having set men over different Churches with Apostolical authority, to preside during their absence, and to succeed them after their decease. This sufficiently appears from places in St. Paul's Epistles to Timothy and Titus."

"Do you remember any of the passages," I asked him.

"I cannot," he said, "call to mind chapter and verse, but I have with me a little paper of memorandums which I use at the school, and which, if it be not loo much trouble, I will thank you to look at,"

The paper was as follows:—for I thought it well to copy what he had written into my pocket memorandum-book.

It appears that Timothy had authority at Ephesus to check false or unedifying Teachers. 1 Tim. i. 3, 4;— to select persons proper to be ordained Bishops, iii. 1–7;—and also Deacons, iii. 8–13.

That he should have particular regard to the Elders who rule well. v. 17.

That he should be cautious of receiving accusations against Elders, v. 19.

That if any [Elders] were convicted it was his duty to reprimand them publicly. v. 20.

That in his decisions he should be strictly impartial. v. 21.

That he should be very cautious on whom he laid his hands. v. 22

That Timothy was in a station, which even the rich and great might respect. vi. 17.

That Timothy had been ordained by St. Paul himself, once, if not twice. 2 Tim. i. 6.

That at his ordination or consecration there was something remarkable in the *Sermon.* 1 Tim. iv. 14. i. 18.

That he was to commit what he had heard from St. Paul to faithful men, who should be able to pass it on to others. 2 Tim. ii. 2.

That Titus had authority to set in order what was wanting in the Cretan Church; Tit. i. 5: and to ordain Bishops in every city; i. 5, 7.

That he was to be cautious whom he selected for this office, i. 6–9.

That he should rebuke false teachers sharply, i. 13.

That if Titus *himself* was a pattern of good works and a teacher of truth, *the whole Church* would gain credit. ii. 7, 8.

That he should rebuke with all authority, ii. 15.

That he should suffer no man to despise him. ii. 15.

That after one or two admonitions he should reject heretical persons. iii. 10.

"Now, Sir, it seems to me evident, from these and others similar passages, that there were certainly in the Church, *as far as the Testament History reaches*, 3 different ranks or orders of Ministers, one above the other."

"It is plainly so," I said.

"But," said he, "there was one point which rather perplexed me, and I was some time before I could make out such an explanation of it as was satisfactory to myself."

"What was that," I asked.

"Why," said he, "it was this. I considered that any person to whom the Apostles granted apostolical authority, (Timothy, for instance,) was from that time higher than a Presbyter or Bishop, and yet could not properly be called an Apostle. What then could he be called? I at last remembered a place in Bishop Wilson's little book, which led me to reflect, that surely as there were Angels, (whether it might mean guardians, or heavenly messengers, or missionary Bishops, as we might say,) of the seven Churches in Asia,—so Timothy might have been called the Angel of the Ephesian Church; and Titus, of the Church of Crete; and the same in other cases. And it came into my thoughts, that, perhaps, after St. John's decease, whether out of humility, or because, (the Churches being settled,) the ministers need no longer be missionaries, the title of Apostles or Angels was laid aside, and that of Bishops limited to the highest of the three orders.

Thus I seemed to myself everywhere to have traced the three-fold order, down from the beginning of the Gospel; the authority and distinction peculiar to each being preserved, a difference in name only taking place.

Thus at first they were	Apostles, Elders, Deacons.
After the decease of some of the Apostles, or at least, while St John was yet living	Angels, Bishops, Deacons.
At some period, after St. John's decease	Bishops, Priests, Deacons.

"I do not see how, what you have said, can be contradicted," I replied.

"But," he proceeded, "there is one thing I must, Sir, confess to you, and it is this;—that I have often said to myself, what a comfort it would be, if it had pleased GOD to preserve to us some few writings of the good men who lived close after the Apostles, that so we might have known their opinion on matters of this kind: and we might have known, too, by what names *they* distinguished the different orders of Ministers, one from another. For, surely, what they would think most proper in such cases, must be safest of all rules for us to follow; unless, (which is a thing not to be supposed,) *their* rules should be contrary to those of the Apostles, as set down in Scripture. So, Sir, I have often thought, if any such writings could be found, what a precious treasure they would be."

"What," said I, "Richard, did you never hear of those who are called the Apostolic Fathers: Clement, Polycarp, Ignatius?"

"I believe I have heard of them," he answered; "but I observed, that you, Sir, and other Clergymen, scarcely ever notice them in your Sermons; and the man I mentioned just now told me that, Mr. Cartwright, who is the minister of the Independent Chapel at the Town, and who is reckoned to be a very learned man and an admired preacher,—that he should say in a Sermon, that the works of the Fathers were very imperfect, and their opinion not much to be trusted to."

"But," said I, "Richard, if a person, whose word you could take, were to shew you an old book written by persons who had seen our SAVIOUR; who had heard St. John and St. Paul preach, and had been well acquainted with them; should you not value such a book, and wish to know whether there was any thing in it, which could throw light on the history of those early times of the Church, and especially with reference to the subjects you and I have been now conversing on?"

"Indeed, Sir, I should," he said. "But if what Mr. Cartwright said is true, it is too much to expect that any such treasure should be found by us."

"No, Richard," I said, "it is not too much. The kind Prodence of GOD has permitted some of the writings of those good men to be preserved to this day. And there is no more doubt that they are their genuine writings, than that Bishop Ken wrote the Evening Hymn, or Bishop Wilson that little book you like so much."

"If this is indeed as you say," he replied, "we have great reason to be thankful for such a proof of GOD's care for His Church. But I beg you, Sir, to tell me, whether there is any thing in these writings you speak of, which confirms what I have been venturing to state to you as my opinion gathered from Scripture, concerning the threefold distinction of Christian Ministers."

"Next Sunday," said I, "you shall see and judge for yourself."

As we came home from Church in the afternoon of the following Sunday, he reminded me of my promise; and I gave him a written paper, containing a few extracts, which I had translated from the works of the Apostolical Fathers, telling him, that I might possibly have made a mistake here and there in the rendering, but that he might depend on such being the general force and meaning of the passages.

The Extracts I gave him were the following:—

"Clement, with other my fellow labourers."—*Phil. iv. 3.*

"Ignatius and the holy Polycarp, the Bishop of the Smyrmæans, had formerly been disciples of the holy

Apostle John."—*Martyrdom of S. Ignatius.*

"The Apostles, preaching throughout countries and cities, used to appoint their first fruits, after they had proved them by the Spirit, to be Bishops and Deacons of those who should hereafter believe."—*S. Clement to the Cor.*

"The Apostles knew that there will be dispute about the name of Bishoprick or Episcopacy, wherefore they appointed the aforementioned, and gave them authority beforehand, in order that if themselves should fall asleep, other approved men might succeed to their ministerial office."—*The same.*

"All of you follow the Bishop as JESUS CHRIST followed the FATHER; and the Presbytery as the Apostles; and reverence the Deacons as God's ordinance. Let no man do any of those things which pertain to the Church without the Bishop. He that honoureth the Bishop, is honoured of GOD; he that doeth any thing without the privity of the Bishop, doeth service to the Devil."—*S. Ignat. to the Smyrm.*

"Have regard to the Bishop, that GOD also may regard you. My soul for theirs who are subject to the Bishops, Elders, and Deacons; and may it be my lot to have a portion with them in GOD."—*S. Ignat. to Polycarp.*

"The Bishops who were appointed in the farthest regions are according to the will of JESUS CHRIST; whence it becometh you to go along with the will of the Bishop."—*S. Ignat. to the Ephes.*

"That ye may obey the Bishop and the Presbytery,

having your mind without distraction, breaking one bread."—*The same.*

"Some indeed talk of the Bishop, yet do every thing without him: but such persons do not appear to me conscientious; on account of their congregations not being assembled strictly according to the commandment."—*S. Ignat. to the Magnes.*

"I exhort you to be zealous to do all things in divine concord: the Bishop presiding in the place of God, and the Presbyters in the place of the council of Apostles, and the Deacons, (in whom I most delight,) intrusted with the service of Jesus Christ."—*The same.*

"For as many as are GOD's and JESUS CHRIST's, these are with the Bishop."—*S. Ignat. to the Philadelph.*

"Be ye earnest to keep one Eucharist, for the flesh of our Lord Jesus Christ is one, and there is one cup in the unity of His blood, one altar, as one Bishop, together with the Presbytery, and Deacons, my fellow-servants."—*The same.*

"Hold to the Bishop, and to the Presbytery, and Deacons. Without the Bishop do nothing."—The same.

"When you are subject to the Bishop as to JESUS CHRIST, ye appear to me as living not according to man's rule, but according to JESUS CHRIST."—*S. Ignat. to the Trail.*

"He that without the Bishop, and Presbytery, and Deacon, doeth ought, that person is not pure in his conscience."—*The same.*

"Polycarp, and the Presbyters, who are with him, to the Church of GOD, sojourning at Philippi."—*S. Polyc. to the Philipp.*

"Being subject to the Presbyters☐Deacons, as to GOD and CHRIST."—*The same.*

Two or three weeks afterwards, as we were walking homewards after Evening Service, he gave me back the paper, with expressions of great satisfaction and thankfulness; and added, that he blessed God for having led him to make the enquiry; and that he was sure, if many religiously-disposed persons, who now think little of such matters, would turn their minds to them without partiality, they would fear to separate from a Church like ours, which, whatever may be its imperfections, is substantially pure in its doctrine, and in the Apostolical Succession of its Ministry.

"Sir," said he, "I am a poor hard-working man, as you know: but the interests of my soul and of those dear to me, are of as great importance in the sight of Almighty GOD, and ought to be to me also, as if my lot had been cast in a higher station. It is to me, therefore, no matter of indifference, (as many have told me it should be,) what is the truth on these great subjects; but I am more and more sure that it is a Christian duty first to enquire into them, and, when we have found the truth, to act up to it, humbly but resolutely.

"The times are bad, I confess; but yet, young though I am, I do not expect, as the world now goes, to see them much better.

"What our LORD said about iniquity abounding, and love growing cold, seems to be but too suitable to our present slate. I have often thought it and said it, though I have seldom met with any one who would agree with me in the opinion. The Church *of* England I can plainly see, more plainly perhaps than a person in a higher station, is in a manner gone. The Church *in* England, GOD be thanked, however afflicted, remains, and ever will, I trust,—whether the world smiles or frowns upon her.

"I have therefore determined, Sir, by GOD's grace, to look to myself, my wife, and children; and not to trust the world to do us any good, either in time, or in Eternity.

"And if by following THE TRUTH now, we shall all be together hereafter in the Society of Prophets, Apostles, Saints, and Martyrs, you know then, Sir, we shall have nothing more to wish for, nothing more to fear; every doubt will be satisfied, every difficulty removed. And I assure you, Sir, it is the very comfort of my life to spend a portion of every Sunday, in looking forward to that happy time."

"God bless you, Richard," said I, "as we parted at his garden gate." And, when I came home, I could not but fall on my knees and thank God for having given me such a Parishioner.

Appendix II – Society of Sacrificial Giving

The motives which have given rise to the Society – its rules and regulations.

It is proposed with the blessing of God that twenty private Christians should unite in laying by a certain annual sum for the five years next ensuing, for the purpose of erecting a Church in some part of England, where it shall be judged most desirable.

The details of the plan, as regards situation and structure, to be agreed upon after mature consideration, and to be decided by the unanimous voice of the whole number of contributors (see Rules).

The motives of this undertaking are:-

1. The glory of God our Saviour, upon whom alone we rely to prevent us in this our design with His most gracious favour, and to further us throughout it with His continual help, that so begun, continued and ended in Him, we may thereby glorify His Holy Name.

2. Our heart-felt conviction of the pressing and immediate necessities of the Church, which call loudly to every Christian in the land to come forward with full purpose of heart, and assist to his uttermost in providing the means of grace, and the benefits of our Holy Church, to the tens of thousands of her baptized members who are at this day wholly deprived of her consolations.

3. Our desire in some degree to imitate those great

works of devotion, so frequently exhibited to us by Christians of ancient times, who did not, as in our days content themselves with forming Societies, large indeed and highly useful in themselves, but to which the individual contributions are commonly meagre, and scarcely missed from our abundance; but who rather come forward as private men, devoting their whole time and fortunes to some grand religious edifice or foundation to God's glory, and to the good of His Church – we who in Oxford are enjoying the fruits of such pious labours, while we have especial reason, daily and hourly to bless God who put the good desire into the hearts of our forefathers, ought to need no further incentives to copy, be it ever so humbly, their bright examples.

4. Our wish to stimulate and encourage among ourselves, the formation of *stricter* habits of *self-denial* that by abridging our daily luxuries and even comforts, we may have the more to spend to God's glory, *who gave them to us*; remembering always the solemn account we shall one day have to render of whatever portion of wealth or other talents He has entrusted to our disposal. That this important object may be better answered, the sum to be contributed by each, should be such as to imply some care and thought, some trouble and inconvenience to ourselves, not ordinarily undertaken in our works of charity, and evincing our heart to be in the cause. The sum of £20 per annum, or £100 in the 5 years, may perhaps be mentioned as the lowest admissible leaving it of course, to the conscience of each to advance as much more than this, as he has ability according

to the measure of abundance with which God has blessed him.

5. Our hope that our example and the sight of the Church when erected might be the means, under God's blessing of influencing others to dedicate a larger portion of their substance to God's service than has been common hitherto, and thereby of stirring up in the country a more bountiful as well as a more personal spirit of liberality.

6. While we look for no other reward on earth than the happiness of seeing our design accomplished, and acknowledge that it is only our bounded duty and service to Him Who has given us all we possess; yet we trust that for Christ's sake it will be accepted and blessed that we shall have treasure laid up in heaven, and that what is now done in secret, the Lord will one day reward openly.

N.B. Our object, it may be suggested, will be better advanced if we confine ourselves to a small number of contributors as is consistent with the amount requisite for our design, that thus we lose not its privacy and individuality.

It is also much to be wished that we should not content ourselves with the cheapest and plainest structure possible, but rather desiring to make it substantial, beautiful and handsomely adorned, in the spirit of David who would not give to God "of that which cost him nothing" and of Solomon who thought nothing too precious to be lavished on God's Temple.

A Resolution might at once be entered into, that whether we are able to endow the Church at the time of its erection, or at any subsequent period; the presentation should immediately and for ever be vested in the hands of the Bishop of the Diocese in which it is built.

Rules

1. That the Patronage of the Church which it is the object of the contributions to build, if endowed, be for ever vested in the hands of the Bishop of the Diocese, and till endowed, in the hands of the Incumbent of the Parish.

2. That the number of Contributors be limited to twenty at a time.

3. That no Contributor shall pay less than £20 per annum during the five years.

4. That each Contributor pay in as much more than £20 as he thinks proper, only anonymously.

5. That a Treasurer be appointed, and that he have a casting vote.

6. That each Contributor may have his money returned to him at any time upon conscientious scruples as to the application of the funds.

7. That business shall be transacted by the members in Oxford while there are as many as five resident, without consulting non-residents, except on emergent occasions, or the alteration of the Rules.

8. That 5 members form a quorum while there are so many resident.

9. That when non-residents are consulted Proxies be admitted.

That subscriptions be paid to Parsons & Co, Oxford, or Hammersley's, Pall Mall, to the account of F. Menzies, B.N.C., the treasurer - in each case specifying the name of the subscriber if it be the regular yearly payment, or the letter [64]which belongs to him if it be anonymous.

The money is invested in the 3p.c. funds under the names of F. Menzies, Rev. W.H. Burrows, Rev. W. H. Ridley.

---

[64] It seems that each of the Contributors was assigned a code name, a letter.

Appendix III - Letter opposing the ordination of Women

To The Most Reverend and Right Hon the Lord Archbishop of Canterbury & The Most Reverend and Right Hon the Lord Archbishop of York

July, 2008

Most Reverend Fathers in God,

We write as bishops, priests and deacons of the Provinces of Canterbury and York, who have sought, by God's grace, in our various ministries, to celebrate the Sacraments and preach the Word faithfully; to form, nurture and catechise new Christians; to pastor the people of God entrusted to our care; and, through the work of our dioceses, parishes and institutions, to build up the Kingdom and to further God's mission to the world in this land. Our theological convictions, grounded in obedience to Scripture and Tradition, and attentive to the need to discern the mind of the whole Church Catholic in matters touching on Faith and Order, lead us to doubt the sacramental ministry of those women ordained to the priesthood by the Church of England since 1994. Having said that, we have engaged with the life of the Church of England in a myriad of ways, nationally and locally, and have made sincere efforts to work courteously and carefully with those with whom we disagree. In the midst of this disagreement over Holy Order, we have, we believe, borne particular witness to the cause of Christian unity, and to the imperative of Our Lord's command that 'all may be one.'

We include those who have given many years' service to the Church in the ordained ministry, and others who are very newly ordained. We believe that we demonstrate the vitality of the tradition which we represent and which has formed us in our discipleship and ministry – a tradition which, we believe, constitutes an essential and invaluable part of the life and character of the Church of England, without which it would be deeply impoverished.

Since the ordination of women to the priesthood began in 1994, we have been able to exercise our ministry in the context of the solemn assurances given at that time that our understanding of Holy Order was one entirely consonant with the faith and practice of the Church of England, and secure in the knowledge that those assurances were embodied in the legislation passed in 1993, and in the Act of Synod which followed that legislation. That legislation, together with the Act, has been the framework which has allowed us to continue to live and work in a church which has taken the decision to allow women to be ordained, but which has also made room for us, and honoured our beliefs and convictions. We have been further encouraged and affirmed by the Resolution of the Lambeth Conference 1998, endorsed by the General Synod in July 2006, that "those who dissent from as well as those who assent to the ordination of women to the priesthood and episcopate are both loyal Anglicans."

We believe that, should the Church of England move to the ordination of women to the episcopate, our ability to continue to minister in the church to which we have been called will depend on provision being made to allow us to do so with the same theological integrity which we have been able to hold since 1994. We recognise that, much as we might hope things to be otherwise, the Church of England is set upon the path of ordaining women as bishops. We will strive to honour their calling as ministers of the Gospel, and to respect the offices which they will hold, despite our profound reservations about the Church of England's decision to ordain and consecrate them. We do not look for 'protection' from the ministry of ordained women. Rather, we ask that our theological convictions continue to be accorded that respect which was promised fifteen years ago. We believe that priests must be able to look to bishops about whose ministry they can be assured; and that bishops in turn must be able to carry out their ministry in a way consonant with the traditional exercise of Episcopal office. Only a structural solution to the new problems which will inevitably be created for the Church by the ordination of women to the episcopate can, we believe, allow us to flourish and to contribute to the life of the whole Church as we believe the Spirit continues to call us to do.

It is with sadness that we conclude that, should the Church of England indeed go ahead with the ordination of women to the episcopate, without at the same time making provision which offers us real ecclesial integrity and security, many of us will be thinking very hard about the way ahead. We will inevitably be asking whether we can, in conscience, continue to minister as bishops, priests and deacons in the Church of England which has been our home. We do not write this in a spirit of making threats or throwing down gauntlets. Rather, we believe that the time has come to make our concerns plain, so that the possible consequences of a failure to make provision which allows us to flourish and to grow are clear.

Your Graces will know that the cost of such a choice would be both spiritual and material.

We know that all members of the Church of England and of the General Synod in particular, will be looking to you for wisdom, guidance and leadership in this matter. We urge you, as our Fathers in God, to lead the whole Church in making generous and coherent provision for us. This will not only allow us to continue to play our part in that mission, under God, to which we are all committed, but also ensure that the Church of England continues to encompass, in her polity, an understanding of Holy Orders consonant with that of the great Churches of East and West with whom we share the historic episcopate.

We assure you of our prayers at this time.

Bibliography

Bright, Michael H, *English Literary Romanticism and the Oxford Movement (Journal of the History of Ideas, vol. 40, no. 3 (Jul - Sept 1979) pp 385-404, University of Pennsylvania Press)*

Defoe Daniel, *A Tour Through the Whole Island of Great Britain* (ed Pat Rogers) (Penguin, London, 1971 – first published London 1714-6)

Fendley John (ed), Bishop Benson's Survey of the Diocese of Gloucester 1735-1750 (J W Arrowsmith, Ltd Bristol, The Bristol & Gloucestershire Archaeological Society, 2000)

Johnston, J A, *St Michael and All Angels Bussage: 1846-1946* (The Stroud News Publishing Co Ltd, Stroud, 1946)

Lambert M D & Shipman J, *The Unknown Cotswold Village: Eastcombe 1500-1980* (University of Reading, 1981)

Lambert M D, *Saint Michael and All Angels Bussage 1846-1986 (1986 ??)*

Lipson E, *The History of the Woollen and Worsted Industries* (A & C Black Ltd, London, 1921)

Mills, Stephen, *The Origins, Development, Decline and Reuse of the Cloth Mills of the Stroud Valleys of Gloucestershire: a Study in Industrial Archaeology* (University of Leicester, Nov. 1997)

Rudd, Mary A, *Historical Records of Bisley with Lypiatt Gloucestshire* (John Jennings, Gloucestershire, 1937)

Summary of Parliamentary report

Thompson E P, *The History of the Working Class*
Urdank, Albion M, Custom, Conflict and Traditional
Authority in the Gloucester Weaver Strike of 1825
(Journal of British Studies, Vol. 25, no. 2 (Apr. 1986)
pp 193-226)

Williams, Rev'd Isaac, A Short Memoir of The Rev'd
Robert Albert Suckling M.A.   (London, 1853)

Online Resources

https://btsarnia.org/2014/06/01/the-oxford-movement-in-gloucestershire/
 15/03/2017 20.17 GMT   Author - Rev. Brian Torode

http://livesonline.rcseng.ac.uk/biogs/E003785b.htm
16/03/2017 19.13 GMT   Biographical Entry Henry
Arnott - Royal College of Surgeons

http://churchdb.gukutils.org.uk/GLS95.php
16/03/2017 19.45 GMT

http://www.puseyhouse.org.uk/what-was-the-oxford-movement.html
27/03/2017 12.10 GMT

http://stroud-textile.org.uk/history/background-to-the-local-wool-industry/
12.36 06/02/2017

https://en.wikipedia.org/wiki/Tracts_for_the_Times

19/07/2017 12.20 GMT

http://anglicanhistory.org/africa/za/jarmstrong1857/
18 May 2017 10.57 Athens time

https://www.chalfordparishlocalhistorygroup.org.uk

Other Materials

1841 Census data obtained from Stroud Library resources.

Bussage Magazine 1895 – 1911 – bound copy of the monthly magazines, generously loaned by Peter Clissold.

Archives of the Stroud Free Press accessed at Stroud Library

About the Author

Other historical/academic works by Patricia Main:

John Moore Chronicler of Country Life – a monograph on the writer and broadcaster John Moore of Tewkesbury

An Ordinary Type of Bloke – the memoir of his experiences in the trenches of the First World War by William Leaver, a London lad

Patricia also writes fiction as Patricia Ainger.

You can find her on Facebook – **Patricia Ainger – Writer**. She loves to hear from readers and always replies to messages received.

She also has a website: **www.patricia-ainger.com** where you may find details both about her and her novels.

Printed in Great Britain
by Amazon